WORKING ON THE PLAY
AND THE ROLE

Irina and Igor Levin

WORKING ON THE PLAY AND THE ROLE

The Stanislavsky Method for Analyzing
the Characters in a Drama

Ivan R. Dee

CHICAGO

WORKING ON THE PLAY AND THE ROLE. Copyright ©
1992 by Irina and Igor Levin. All rights reserved, including the
right to reproduce this book or portions thereof in any form.
For information, address: Ivan R. Dee, Inc., 1332 North Hal-
sted Street, Chicago 60622. Manufactured in the United
States of America and printed on acid-free paper.

Library of Congress Cataloging-in-Publication Data:
Levin, Irina.
    Working on the play and the role : the Stanislavsky
method for analyzing the characters in a drama / Irina and
Igor Levin.
        p.   cm.
    Includes bibliographical references and index.
    ISBN 0-929587-94-4 (acid-free paper). —
    ISBN 0-929587-93-6 (pbk. acid-free paper)
    1. Method (Acting). 2. Chekhov, Anton Pavlovich, 1860–
1904. Vishnevyĭ sad. 3. Chekhov, Anton Pavlovich, 1860–
1904—Characters. 4. Characters and characteristics in liter-
ature. I. Levin, Igor. II. Title.
    PN2062.L48   1992
    792'.028—dc20   92-3054

CONTENTS

Introduction   7

Part One. Analyzing a Play

1. Conflicts and Actions   15
2. Example I   16
3. Example II   22
4. Example III   24
5. Aspects of a Conflict   26
6. On the Internal Logic of the Text   28
7. Events   28
8. Breaking a Play Down into Events   29
9. Groups   30
10. Example IV   30
11. Incidental Conflicts   32
12. Example V   32
13. Interrupted Events   34
14. Description of Actions   35
15. On the Monologue   35
16. Summary   36

Part Two. Analysis of The Cherry Orchard

17. Characters in the Play   41
18. Act I   46
19. Act II   87
20. Act III   113
21. Act IV   138

Part Three. The Superobjective of the Character

22. The Concept of the Superobjective   *161*
23. Superobjectives of *The Cherry Orchard* Characters   *163*
24. On Staging a Play   *172*

Conclusion   *173*

Appendices   *175*

Bibliography   *183*

Index   *185*

Introduction

"MY SO-CALLED 'SYSTEM,'" wrote Konstantin Stanislavsky, "is the result of lifelong searchings. I have groped after a method of work for actors which will enable them to create the image of a character, breathe into it the life of a human spirit, and, by natural means, embody it on the stage in a beautiful artistic form." In Stanislavsky's view the actor must always remain a living person on the stage—in other words, he must sincerely feel, think, and act in the circumstances presented by the role, following the logic of life and the laws of human nature.

The true emotions of an actor, as well as that creative uplift called inspiration without which there is no art, do not appear on order. Traditional methods of theatrical art offered the actor an extensive range of cut-and-dried technical devices for depicting joy, grief, hatred, embarrassment, and other emotions. Stanislavsky called all those methods of conventional representation of emotions and characters theatrical clichés, which have nothing in common with the genuine art of emotion. Stanislavsky's entire system is aimed at investigating the inner causes and logic of originating emotions, at finding ways of leading the actor to a natural emotional state on the stage. He proposed that things which in real life appear and occur "of their own accord," that is, spontaneously and naturally, be recreated on the stage by means of acting techniques specially designed by him.

"The subconscious through the conscious, the spontaneous

7

through the deliberate," is how he explained the essence of acting technique. "First of all, it is necessary to create consciously and truthfully. This provides the best basis for the origination of the subconscious and inspiration." Stanislavsky accordingly subdivided his system into two major parts: "the actor's work on himself" and "the actor's work on the role."

"The actor's work on himself" sets forth a consistent method of shaping an actor's technique and preparing him for the artistic effort of creating a stage character. Stanislavsky pointed out that without a well-developed imagination, emotional memory, stable concentration, and on-stage communication; without faith, truth, and logic in on-stage behavior, and a number of other elements of the system, an actor is incapable of feeling naturally and thereby creating a full-blooded character.

Creativity, Stanislavsky believed, is a psycho-physical process. At the moment of creativity, he writes, "there develops an interaction of body and soul, of actions and emotions, thanks to which the external helps the internal, and the internal evokes the external." He developed an acting technique aimed entirely at ensuring that the action on stage, occurring within the circumstances of the play, retains all the characteristics of genuine, living action occurring in life.

Stanislavsky set forth his ideas on the actor's "work on himself" in two volumes, published shortly after his death in 1938. Both were translated into English and are widely known under the titles *An Actor Prepares*[1]* and *Building a Character*.[2] Elements of Stanislavsky's system may also be found in most textbooks on acting technique.

The second part of Stanislavsky's system deals with the creative process of working on the play and the role. In order to create a living character on the stage, the actor needs more than perfect mastery of all the elements of acting technique. He must work on the play in a manner that will enable him to understand the meaning of each of the roles com-

*The superior figures refer to items in the Bibliography, page 183.

prising it, and the nature of the relations between these roles. Stanislavsky developed his methods of working on the play and the role over many years. This part of his system remained unfinished, mainly because he continued his search until the very end, continually expanding, improving, and changing the methods of work on the play by verifying them on stage in practice. Several times Stanislavsky began to write about the actor's work on the role, but each time he paused because his ideas had evolved. This is why the relevant materials from his archive, which were published in 1957, are no more than isolated chapters, fragments, and notes relating to different periods in the development of that part of his system. An English translation of those materials is known under the title, *Creating a Role*.[3]

Stanislavsky never described his later findings, and they are known only as recounted by his pupils and associates of those years. His closest associate, M. Kedrov (subsequently the Moscow Art Theater's artistic director), wrote that only the few who had worked with Stanislavsky on his staging of *Tartuffe* (1937–1938) were familiar with his new approach to work on the role.[4] After Stanislavsky's death that approach, later called "the method of active analysis," was expanded and perfected in actual theater work by leading Russian directors and actors. In spite of this, there remains no systematic outline of the method. It is described in only a few papers, stenographic reports of seminars, and notes kept by leading Russian directors during their work on individual plays.[4-12] All of these materials are fragmentary and offer no idea of the method as a whole.

The purpose of this book is to provide a full and systematic explanation of the method of work on a play. Our interpretation of the method is based chiefly on the work of the outstanding Russian directors M. N. Kedrov and G. A. Tovstonogov. Another source is the directing seminars of Professor A. Katsman of the Leningrad Theater Institute, in which one of the authors participated in 1970–1974.

9

*

It is meaningless to describe the method of work on a play without referring to specific dramaturgic material. No extent of general discourse or recommendations about working on a play can bring the reader a step closer to understanding the essence of the method, still less of how to apply it in practice. Moreover, it is impossible fully to grasp the essence of the method by offering examples of its application to only parts of a play; an analysis of the entire play is essential. We have selected for such an analysis Chekhov's *The Cherry Orchard*, which, in the words of at least one critic, is "perhaps the most beautiful and certainly the most complex play of our time, and the most influential in shaping the course of modern drama."[13] This play is ideal material for our purpose because of the complexity of the genre and the psychology of its characters, making it possible to present fully and comprehensively both the essence and specific features of the method.

Work on a play requires continuous reference to the author's text. Regardless of how well the reader knows it, he must constantly have the text before his eyes. That is why the text of the play is an essential component of this book. The text of *The Cherry Orchard* used here is taken from the well-known translation—in our view, one of the most faithful—by Constance Garnett. We urge the reader to read the play carefully (in any translation) before proceeding with the basic sections of this book.

*

This book consists of three main parts. Part One sets forth the basic theoretical principles of work on the play and the role. It begins with a definition of the concepts and terms employed. We introduce such concepts as "conflict," "action," and "leading character," and, with specific examples taken from the play, explain the sense in which they are understood in this book. These concepts make it possible to represent the play as a succession of "events"—logically independent units, each of which has one leading character involved in only one conflict, and one action. This succession of events becomes the objective basis for the subsequent analysis of the play.

In Part Two, the general concepts and principles examined in Part One are applied to our analysis of *The Cherry Orchard*. This part consists of five chapters. The first provides a synopsis of the principal facts and circumstances in the lives of the play's characters prior to the opening scenes. The next four chapters are devoted to analyzing the corresponding acts of the play. Each chapter includes the relevant text of the play presented as a sequence of events. The text of each event is followed by its analysis. The play includes 107 such events.

The reader may also use Part Two as a handbook for practical exercises in the workshop environment. For this purpose we provide each event with brief directorial advice and suggestions for props, details of costumes, and small sets.

Part Three examines one of the least developed concepts of Stanislavsky's system: the *superobjective* of the character. Stanislavsky pointed out that in a play each character has an overall objective or main desire which conditions the character's behavior throughout the entire play. This desire, which Stanislavsky called "the superobjective of the character," welds together all the parts of the role and determines how it evolves in the direction envisioned by the author. It is extremely important for the actor to know the superobjective of his character, as this enables him to create an integral and purposeful theatrical character.

Despite the great practical importance of the superobjective concept, to this day there is no clear understanding of what it represents, still less of how to identify it. In Part Three we show the close connection between the conflicts and actions of a character and his superobjective; we explain the meaning of the superobjective and offer a practical method of defining it. We then go on to present the superobjectives of all the play's characters and show that they derive directly from the analysis of the play in Part Two. At the end of the book are appendices containing additional notes relevant to *The Cherry Orchard* as well as our recommendations for exploring the method in a workshop environment.

We should like to thank Vladimir Talmy, Eugene Levin, and Dr. Angelo J. Skalafuris for their help in preparing this book for publication. We also thank Professor William J. Bruehl, State University of New York at Stony Brook, for his valuable criticisms.

I. and I. L.

Washington, D.C.
January 1992

WORKING ON THE PLAY
AND THE ROLE

PART ONE

Analyzing a Play

1. Conflicts and Actions

STANISLAVSKY CLAIMED THAT an actor can be "living a part" only when he seeks to communicate with his partners, when he strives to influence them and is influenced by them. Thus Stanislavsky regarded the actor's performance on the stage primarily as a process of live interaction. This interaction must be based on the relations between the characters given by the author, in other words, on the material of the play.

In order to reveal those relations, Stanislavsky suggests treating the play as a continuous process of struggle between the characters to achieve their objectives. Each character participates in a continuous series of confrontations or, as we shall call them, *conflicts* with other characters. In each *conflict* the character adopts a specific pattern of behavior or *action* which should, in his opinion, ensure success over his "opponent."

In daily life the words *conflict* and *action* are used in a broad and often vague sense. To avoid possible uncertainty and confusion, we use these words in one sense only, and solely as special terms. The conflicts we shall examine are based on the way the characters perceive one another. So the focal point of a conflict can only be one of its participants, not some circumstance, object, or idea. Every conflict has one side which originates and sustains it, not allowing it to peter out. We call this the *leading* side. Correspondingly, the opposite side is called the *led* side. Each side actively strives to "remake" its opponent in its own likeness, subordinate the other side to its own will, and thereby force on that side its own point of view. In the course of the psychological confrontation, each side resorts to a tactic aimed at influencing the other side. That is what we call the *action*.

2. Example I

In order better to understand what lies behind the words *conflict* and *action* and how to identify them, we turn to specific dramaturgic material. Our first example is the scene of the meeting between Anya and Dunyasha in Act I of *The Cherry Orchard*. The text of this scene follows.

DUNYASHA: We've been expecting you so long.... *[Takes Anya's hat and coat]*

ANYA: I haven't slept for four nights on the trip.... I feel dreadfully cold.

DUNYASHA: You set out in Lent, there was snow and frost, and now? My darling! *[Laughs and kisses her]* I have missed you, my precious, my joy.... I must tell you at once, I can't put off a minute....

ANYA: *[Wearily]* Again something....

DUNYASHA: The clerk, Epihodov, proposed to me just after Easter.

ANYA: It's always the same subject with you.... *[Fixing her hair]* I've lost all my hairpins. *[She is staggering from exhaustion]*

DUNYASHA: I don't know what to think, really. He does love me, he does love me so!

ANYA: *[Looking towards her door, tenderly]* My own room, my windows just as though I had never gone away. I'm home! Tomorrow morning I shall get up and run into the garden.... Oh, if I could get to sleep! I haven't slept all the journey, I was so anxious and worried.

DUNYASHA: Pyotr Sergeyevitch came the day before yesterday.

ANYA: *[Joyfully]* Petya!

DUNYASHA: He sleeps in the bath house, he has settled in there. I'm afraid to be a bother, says he. *[Glancing at her watch]* I was to have waked him, but Varvara Michailovna told me not to. Don't wake him, says she.

[Enter Varya with a bunch of keys at her waist]

VARYA: Dunyasha, coffee and make haste.... Mamma's asking for coffee.

DUNYASHA: This very minute. *[Goes out]*

a. Given Circumstances

Conflicts between characters do not appear out of nothing; they are rooted in so-called *given circumstances*. Given circumstances include the story of the play, the facts, events, epoch, time, and place of action, supplemented by our imagination. Using the information provided by the author about his characters, we must reconstruct and form an idea of their previous lives. In this we frequently find it necessary to go beyond the framework of the author's story line and conjecture about the characters' lives before the beginning of the play and in the intervals between their appearance on stage. This is why, as a rule, it is impossible to reveal the conflict that exists in an isolated scene taken out of the body of a play. It is necessary to study the play as a whole, for frequently the conflict of a given scene is based on information supplied by the author in other parts of the play and, what's more, through the words of other characters not participating in the scene being considered.

Obviously, not all given circumstances are equally important to determine the conflict in a given scene. In order correctly to identify the conflict it is first necessary to select the given circumstances which condition it—namely, the circumstances which induce the leading character to begin the confrontation, and the circumstances which determine the led character's response. To identify such circumstances we must try to understand how they are perceived by the parties to the conflict; we must view them, as it were, through their own eyes, in their own interpretation. In that case the description of the given circumstances will already contain the logic and mind-set of the corresponding character.

Below are the given circumstances we have selected for Dunyasha and Anya. *Remember that we always aim to present the given circumstances from the standpoint of the respective character.*

b. Given Circumstances for Dunyasha

The maid Dunyasha was taken into the Ranevskaya home as a child and grew up with Anya. They are approximately the same age, and Dunyasha is used to sharing her secrets with Anya. While Anya has been away from home, some unusual events have occurred—the most significant of them is that the clerk Epihodov has fallen madly in love with Dunyasha and made a proposal of marriage to her. Another important event which cannot leave Anya indifferent is the visit of the student Trofimov (Pyotr Sergeyevich), whose company Anya enjoys every summer. Living in a home where there is no one else of her age, Dunyasha is quite miserable because of her forced loneliness. She is delighted with the arrival of Anya, whom she has missed very much. At last there is a person with whom she can share her news and gossip.

c. Given Circumstances for Anya

Seventeen-year-old Anya has returned home after an absence of several months, matured and brimming with new impressions and concerns. Her trip to Paris brought her, for the first time, face to face with the concerns and difficulties of life, with the hitherto unknown world of adults. Having grown up

18

on a elegant country estate, in an atmosphere of loving care and happiness, Anya realizes for the first time what it means to live without money, among strangers in a strange, indifferent house. After five years of separation, Anya has suddenly rediscovered her mother, whom she had grown up without. She finds her mother unhappy, lost, and helpless—she is ruined, and their fine estate may have to be sold to pay debts. Anya is in a state of great distress which has driven her to insomnia. She understands that her family's fate hangs in the balance; now everything depends upon whether her uncle and Varya manage to pay the debts. This is all that concerns Anya now; it fills her thoughts.

d. The Leading Character and the Conflict

To determine the conflict we must first identify the leading character. To do this we must turn to the text of the scene and see which is the active character, the striving party. Apparently, in this scene the active character is Dunyasha, who continues to pester the tired Anya with her talk. She originates and sustains the conflict, which would immediately die without her efforts.

Let us now take the given circumstances for the leading character, Dunyasha, and try to see what causes her activity, why she is so happy that Anya has returned, why she keeps pestering Anya with her talk despite Anya's resistance. The answer that suggests itself is: There is no one in the house closer to Dunyasha in age and interests than Anya. They grew up together, and Dunyasha sees Anya not so much as a mistress but as a friend with whom she has much in common. That is precisely what Dunyasha is imposing, what she is insisting on. That is Dunyasha's side of the conflict.

This point of view immediately arouses Anya's resistance. Turning to the given circumstances for Anya, we understand that her inner world now has nothing in common with Dunyasha's. She will not share with a maid her sorrows and concerns, all that she has experienced over the past months and all that concerns her now.

Thus the conflict between Dunyasha and Anya can be stated as follows: Dunyasha sees Anya as a person close to her, with whom she shares common interests. But Anya, matured and filled with new impressions, no longer finds anything in common with the maid Dunyasha.

At the root of this conflict is a clear difference of opinion about the person of Anya.

e. The Characters' Actions

The next step is to determine the characters' behavioral tactics in this conflict, in other words, identify their actions.

Let us reread the scene and, on the basis of the identified conflict, try to understand what lies behind the characters' words, how they attempt to influence each other. As we see from the text, Dunyasha rushes toward Anya with hugs and chatter. She has no doubt that, although tired, Anya is very happy with their meeting and the opportunity to talk about things of mutual interest. Throughout the scene Dunyasha strives to involve Anya and arouse her interest. That is her line of behavior, her action.

Anya's action, on the other hand, consists in distancing herself from Dunyasha, getting rid of her pestering. We see that first Anya simply refuses to maintain a conversation, showing in every way that Dunyasha's news is of no interest and that she has more important problems of her own. Then, seeing there is no stopping Dunyasha, Anya pointedly turns her attention to the room and the garden. But Dunyasha persists and turns the conversation to what should, in her view, arouse Anya's interest, namely, the arrival of Trofimov. As a result, Anya's resistance weakens, and Dunyasha captures her attention and pours out a torrent of details. Only the appearance of a new given circumstance—the entrance of Varya—causes Dunyasha to interrupt her action.

20

f. Realization of Actions on the Stage

It is impossible to predict how the action will be realized by an actor on stage. The physical realization of an action through the actor's body movements and the mise-en-scène is a highly subjective process. Different actors will perform the same action differently. It depends on an actor's individuality, talent, experience, and, of course, his training and command of the acting technique.

Nonetheless, we offer an idea of how the actions might be realized physically by actors. The reader must bear in mind that the following description is highly subjective and based on our perception of how we would have realized these actions had we been performing ourselves.

To realize her action—to involve Anya and to arouse her interest—Dunyasha physically struggles to keep Anya next to her and to remain in the center of her attention. She takes off Anya's hat and coat, sits her down on the sofa, and upon Anya's complaint of being cold and tired, covers her with a blanket. When Anya says she has lost her hairpins, Dunyasha fixes Anya's hair by taking hairpins out of her own hairdo, just so she will not have to go get them and leave Anya even for a moment. When Anya talks about the garden, the room, and her worries, Dunyasha immediately sits down, hugs her, and tries to regain her attention by mentioning Petya's arrival.

Anya's action—to distance herself from Dunyasha—is physically manifested by not looking at Dunyasha and avoiding the establishment of any contact. Anya constantly turns away from Dunyasha, mentions how tired she is, interrupts, and shifts her attention to the room, the garden, and her hair. But the news of Petya's arrival captivates her so, she forgets everything else and directs her attention at Dunyasha. As a result, Anya is "defeated."

3. Example II

For our second example we have chosen the scene involving Yasha and Dunyasha from Act I.

> [Yasha enters with a rug and a traveling bag]
> YASHA: [Crosses the stage, mincingly] May one come in here, pray?
> DUNYASHA: I wouldn't have recognized you, Yasha. How you have changed abroad.
> YASHA: H'm!... And who are you?
> DUNYASHA: When you went away, I was that high... [Shows distance from the floor] Dunyasha, Fyodor Kozodoev's daughter. You don't remember me!
> YASHA: H'm!... You're a peach! [Looks round and embraces her; she shrieks and drops a saucer. Yasha goes out hastily]

As in the previous example, we begin by describing the given circumstances. Once again we remind the reader that we *always* aim to present the given circumstances from the point of view of the respective character, in his or her own interpretation.

a. Given Circumstances for Dunyasha

In the years she has lived in the Ranevskaya home, Dunyasha has grown unaccustomed to a simple life and, in her own words, has become quite a young lady. She is used to success among the local young men and has no doubts that she is irresistible. The clerk Epihodov, an educated and tactful man, follows her around pleading for her to marry him. But Dunyasha refuses to respond, because she isn't quite sure that he is good enough for her. Seeing the valet Yasha again after several years, Dunyasha is awed by his mannerisms and "foreign" looks. At last a young man who could interest her has appeared here, in the country.

22

b. Given Circumstances for Yasha

Yasha is a young valet who was born and grew up in the same village as Dunyasha. Before his journey abroad he had served in the Ranevskaya home with Dunyasha. In Yasha's opinion, five years in France have made him a different man. He is no longer a part of either the provincial life or the simple, ignorant folk. Nothing here can arouse his interest, everything is a priori disdainful and boring.

c. The Leading Character and the Conflict

From the text we see that Dunyasha is the active, leading character: she starts the conversation with Yasha as he passes by, and she also ends it when she shrieks and drops the saucer.

Proceeding from the given circumstances described above, we can describe the relationship between the characters as follows: Dunyasha sees Yasha as a young man fully up to her standards, an embodiment of her dream. Yasha, for his part, considers that he, a "European," can have nothing in common with a simple country maid.

As we see, the focal point of the conflict is Yasha: his opinion of himself has nothing in common with the way Dunyasha sees him.

d. Actions

Turning to the text, we see that Dunyasha stops Yasha as he passes by and strikes up a flirting conversation, making no secret of her obvious interest in him. It is not hard to see that her action is to show off and attract and captivate him. Yasha's action is to emphasize the distance between them. First he stubbornly "does not recognize" Dunyasha (note that Ranevskaya recognizes her at once—see Event 1.6, page 52), thereby emphasizing how far removed he is from his old milieu. Then, in response to Dunyasha's flirting, Yasha "softens" and finally condescends, unceremoniously embracing her. For Dunyasha, who did not expect such an outcome, there is nothing left but to shriek and drop the saucer—as a real young lady should in such circumstances.

e. Realization of Actions on the Stage

Yasha, stopped in his path, places the blanket and the bag on the armchair, puts in his monocle, and, peering at Dunyasha, presses his advance. Dunyasha does not step back, allowing Yasha to admire her and showing off, in every way, her white hands—those of a "real young lady" which she is so proud of. Yasha comes closer and confidently takes her in his arms. Dunyasha, as if losing consciousness, hangs on to Yasha, cries out, and drops the saucer she is holding. Yasha glances at the door leading to the adjacent room and hastily exits, picking up his things on the way.

4. Example III

For our third example we have chosen the following scene of Yasha and Dunyasha from Act II.

DUNYASHA: I've become so restless, I worry all the time. I was a little girl when I was taken into our lady's house, and now I have quite grown out of peasant ways, and my hands are white, as white as a lady's. I'm such a delicate, sensitive creature, I'm afraid of everything. I'm so frightened. And if you deceive me, Yasha, I don't know what will become of my nerves.

YASHA: [Kisses her] You're a peach! Of course a girl must never forget herself; what I dislike more than anything is a girl being bad in her behavior.

DUNYASHA: I'm passionately in love with you, Yasha; you are a man of culture—you can give your opinion about everything. [A pause]

YASHA: [Yawns] Yes.... My opinion is this: if a girl loves anyone, that means that she has no morals. [A pause] It's pleasant smoking a cigar in the open air. *[Listens]* Someone is coming this way.... It's the gentlefolk.... *[Dunyasha embraces him impulsively]* Go home, as though you had been to the river to bathe; go by the path, or else they'll meet you and suppose I have had a date with you here. I can't stand it.

DUNYASHA: *[Coughing softly]* The cigar has made my head ache....

[Goes off]

a. Given Circumstances for Dunyasha

It is about a month after the scene analyzed in Example II. Dunyasha and Yasha have fallen passionately in love and entered into a relationship. Their affair is at its peak, but Yasha has not proposed. Dunyasha, accustomed to success among the local young men, is quite dismayed. She begins to realize that she has landed in a terrible mess.

b. Given Circumstances for Yasha

Bored by the tediousness of country life, Yasha entered into a love affair with Dunyasha. But he never held out any hope for her, and she can have no claims against him on this score.

(Remember, once more, that the given circumstances are presented from the point of view of the respective character and thus reflect his or her thinking.)

c. The Leading Character and the Conflict

One need but read the passage to see that the active, leading character here is Dunyasha. On the basis of the given circumstances, the relationship between the characters can be described as follows: Dunyasha views herself as an honorable girl who deserves respect and consideration. But to Yasha she is a girl of easy virtue with whom there is no need to stand on ceremony. Thus the conflict is based on a difference of opinion about Dunyasha's character.

d. The Action

On the basis of the established conflict and the text of the scene, we can surmise that Dunyasha's action is to prod Yasha into a frank conversation and determine his future plans. Dunyasha stresses her bewilderment and helplessness, pointing out that Yasha is responsible for the ambiguous situation in which she finds herself.

Yasha's action is to define their relationship. Not only has he no intention of committing himself, he doesn't even want them to be seen together.

e. Realization of Actions on the Stage

Dunyasha clings to Yasha and presses against him as if looking for his protection. Yasha shows with all his demeanor that her words have no relevance to him. He pointedly enjoys the surroundings, smokes a cigar with pleasure, and absentmindedly replies to Dunyasha while yawning and stretching.

(Once again we remind the reader that this realization is highly subjective and reflects only our perception of how the actions might be physically realized.)

5. Aspects of a Conflict

Any confrontation, by its very nature, assumes a point of discord over which an argument begins and develops. In our conflicts that point is always one of the characters involved in the conflict. Accordingly, the essence of the conflict is determined by the difference of opinions about that character.

For example, in the first of the scenes analyzed above the difference arises as a result of different perceptions of Anya: Dunyasha sees her as someone close, sharing the same interests. Anya, for her part, has an entirely different opinion of herself and sees nothing in common with the maid Dunyasha. In the second example the conflict is determined by different perceptions of Yasha: Dunyasha sees him as a young

26

man suitable for her; Yasha, with his "Parisian" airs, thinks he can have nothing in common with a country maid. Finally, in the third example the conflict is determined by different perceptions of Dunyasha: she sees herself as an honorable girl deserving respect, while to Yasha she is a lass of easy virtue with whom no respect is necessary.

Thus only two types of relations are possible between the parties involved in a conflict. In one case the leading character imposes his opinion of himself on the other party. In the other case the leading character states his view of the opposing party. In both cases the leading character strives to overcome the other side's resistance, to "remake him in his own image," to force him to think along his own lines. The opponent resists this and defends his positions.

The selected scenes illustrate both types of relationships between characters. In the first two examples the leading character (Dunyasha) states how she sees her opponent. In the third example the leading Dunyasha declares who she is.

It should be noted that a conflict without a common point of contention is meaningless. In such a case neither character has any cause for confrontation, as no one is challenging the other's opinion.

In our examples only two characters were involved in the conflicts. But in the most general case either side or both sides of the conflict may involve several characters. Later we shall deal in greater detail with such conflicts.

Our definition of a conflict invariably assumes the manifest presence of the two confronting sides, each of which can be represented by one or several characters. This means that, in this book, conflicts do not involve such abstract concepts as "conflict of conscience," "conflict with society," and the like, in which there is no physical opponent. The question of monologues—that is, scenes in which a character is not communicating with anyone—will be discussed later.

6. On the Internal Logic of the Text

The examples above show that conflicts do not appear manifestly in the story of the play. They are always hidden, concealed behind the author's text. Even in those seemingly "obvious" cases when the characters, at the author's direction, engage in open verbal and sometimes even physical confrontation, it is still necessary to identify their conflict and establish their true relations. By taking such an approach to the play, the actor is not left a prisoner of words as the only mode of expression. This means that the actor does not play the plot but probes deep into what is hidden behind the characters' words, into what they have in mind when they speak those words, and the true issues in their confrontations.

7. Events

The scenes analyzed above represent logically complete units of the play. Each contains one conflict, with one leading character, who has only one action. We call such a unit of the play an *event*. This choice of words is not arbitrary; it indicates that that portion of the play describes a complete stage in the relationship between the characters, and develops the plot. We use the word *event* only in this sense.

Every event starts with the beginning of a conflict involving the leading character and ends when the leading character ends his action. It follows that an event can end only in two ways: either the leading character achieves his objective in this conflict, or a new given circumstance appears which forces him to interrupt his action. In either case the event ends with the action of the leading character.

The end of an event does not necessarily mean an end to the given conflict. A play may have several successive events with the same conflict. Moreover, all those events may also have the same leading character if his actions change from event to event. Thus the basic principle of subdividing the play into events is observed: *An event ends when, and only when, the action of the leading character ends.*

8. Breaking a Play Down into Events

In order to reveal the conflicting relationships between the characters of a play, it must be subdivided into a series of successive events. This succession of events can be constructed according to our definition of an event.

The beginning of the first event is always known: it coincides with the beginning of the play. Thus to identify the first event we need only to determine where it ends. For that we must study the given circumstances for the characters prior to the beginning of the play and identify the leading character, his conflict, and his action. The first event ends when the leading character ends his action.

The next step is to identify the second event of the play. The beginning of the event is already known, because the second event begins immediately after the first one ends. To find where it ends, consider the given circumstances up to the beginning of the second event, and determine the leading character, his conflict, and his action. The second event ends when the leading character ends his action. Repeating this procedure, we can successively identify the subsequent events of the play until the entire play is broken down into events.

Many writers—for example, Shakespeare, Ibsen, Tennessee Williams—subdivide their plays into segments called scenes. Although this division is accomplished by the purely formal entrance or exit of a character, some scenes are also events in that they have one conflict, with one leading character performing one action. In general, though, a scene does not coincide with an event, for the entrance or exit of a character does not necessarily signal the end of an event; similarly, a scene may span several events. Nor does an event necessarily begin with the words of the leading character. Quite often an event starts with the words of another character, and these words stimulate the leading character to initiate his conflict.

The segmenting of a play into events is objective in the sense that it reflects the logic of the author and not our interpretation of the play. The sequence of events is contained in the play and provided by the author. Our task is only to bring that sequence to the surface and make the obscure apparent. If two people independently break a play down into events, ideally they should have identical results.

9. Groups

As we have defined an event, it can have only one leading character, which can have only one conflict and one action. Therefore, if the leading side of a conflict consists of several characters, they must all perform in the given conflict as an entity—they must all hold the same position vis-à-vis the opposing side of the conflict and perform the same action. Of such characters we say they form a *group*. We shall repeatedly encounter instances when the sides of a conflict are represented by groups of characters.

The characters belonging to the led side of the conflict must not necessarily form a group. Each one can have his own position in the conflict as well as his own action. This is the case in the scene from Act III of *The Cherry Orchard* presented below.

10. Example IV

DUNYASHA: *[She has stopped to powder herself]* My young lady tells me to dance. There are plenty of gentlemen, and too few ladies, but dancing makes me giddy and makes my heart beat. Firs, the post-office clerk said something to me just now that quite took my breath away.
[Music becomes more subdued]
FIRS: What did he say to you?
DUNYASHA: He said I was like a flower.
YASHA: *[Yawns]* What ignorance.... *[Goes out]*

30

DUNYASHA: Like a flower.... I am a girl of such delicate feelings, I am awfully fond of soft speeches.
FIRS: Your head's being turned.

a. Given Circumstances of the Characters

Two months have passed since the scene examined in Example III. Dunyasha is still in love with Yasha who has noticeably cooled toward her. But today she has a fine opportunity to show him whom he is spurning. There is a ball in the house, at which Dunyasha enjoys tremendous success. Men are jostling to invite her to dance and showering her with compliments.

Yasha is irritated by Dunyasha's stupid boasting. She has begun to think too highly of herself.

Firs is an eighty-seven-year-old servant who has spent his entire life with Ranevskaya's family. The wise Firs knows life, and nothing in the house can escape his experienced eye. It is obvious to him that Dunyasha is in love with Yasha, and to him their true relations are no secret.

b. The Conflict and Actions

Obviously, the leading character here is Dunyasha. The other side of the conflict is represented by two characters, Yasha and Firs. At the center of the conflict is Dunyasha who wishes to impose a certain opinion on the others. Her opponents challenge that opinion, though each one has his own view of Dunyasha.

The conflict: Dunyasha sees herself as a charming young lady, an object of male worship. To Yasha she is only a country maid with nothing special about her. Firs sees Dunyasha as a giddy girl who has embarked on a slippery path.

Dunyasha's action is to fan Yasha's interest in her. By telling Firs of her success among young men, she hopes to make Yasha, who has cooled toward her, jealous. Yasha's action is to put Dunyasha in her place, knock the wind out of her. Firs's action is to forewarn and guide Dunyasha. He openly warns that her behavior will lead to no good.

11. Incidental Conflicts

Conflict relations between characters are not limited to the simplest case of a confrontation between two sides. Besides the main conflict, which determines the beginning and end of an event, an event may also include other conflicts, which we call *incidental*.

In addition to the leading and led sides of the main conflict, an event may include other characters not involved in the main conflict. These *secondary* characters can only be involved in incidental conflicts with the led characters of the main conflict of an event.

During the time a led character is involved in an incidental conflict, he must abandon the main conflict. This involves the appearance of a new point of contention, which may be either the led character himself or a secondary character interacting with him. When the incidental conflict is over, the led character rejoins the main conflict. Thus the principle is observed that a character cannot be simultaneously involved in two conflicts (since he cannot perform more than one action at any given moment). The leading character of the main conflict cannot participate in incidental conflicts, otherwise he would have to end his action in the main conflict, which would signal the end of the event.

In its inner structure an incidental conflict is in every way similar to the main conflict: one side is the leading side, the other is the led side; each side can be represented by one or several characters.

12. Example V

As an example of an event with an incidental conflict, here is the scene of the encounter with the Wayfarer in Act II.

[The Wayfarer appears in a shabby forage cap and an overcoat; he is slightly drunk]
WAYFARER: Allow me to inquire, can I get to the station this way?
GAEV: Yes, go along that road.
WAYFARER: I thank you most feelingly. *[Coughing]* The weather is superb. *[Declaims]* My brother, my suffering brother!... Come out to the Volga! Whose groan do you hear?... *[To Varya]* Mademoiselle, vouchsafe a hungry Russian thirty kopecks....
[Varya utters a shriek of alarm]
LOPAHIN: *[Angrily]* There's a right and a wrong way of doing everything!
RANEVSKAYA: *[Confusedly]* Here, take this.... *[Looks in her purse]* I've no silver.... No matter—here's a gold piece for you....
WAYFARER: I thank you most feelingly! *[Goes off]*

The main conflict involves the Wayfarer (the leading character), Gaev, and a group comprising Lopahin and Varya. The main conflict ends with the Wayfarer's exit. Within this event is an incidental conflict involving a secondary character, Ranevskaya, and one of the led characters of the main conflict, Lopahin. The leading character in the incidental conflict is Ranevskaya.

a. Main Conflict of the Event

Given circumstances of the leading character: The Wayfarer has a stroke of good luck—he stumbles onto a group of partying gentry who doubtlessly will not refuse him a handout.

Given circumstances of Gaev, Varya, and Lopahin: The drunkard is bothering them by forcing a conversation.

Conflict: The Wayfarer sees himself to be a respectable person deserving compassion and concern. But to Gaev, Varya, and Lopahin he is a drunken beggar who needs money for another drink.

Wayfarer's action: to win sympathy and compassion. First

he prepares the ground by asking the way with deliberate politeness. Then, encouraged by the fact that he is actually spoken to, he recites a few words from two popular poems about the victims of social injustice and turns to Varya, who looks like a compassionate nun, to beg her for money.

Gaev's action: to stay aside, not to become involved. Action of Varya and Lopahin: to expose the Wayfarer and chase him off. They are used to dealing with ordinary folk.

b. Incidental Conflict

Lopahin has disgraced them all by rudely attacking an unfortunate person without cause. As a consequence a conflict arises: Ranevskaya considers herself to be put in an awkward position. But to Lopahin she is a naive person, remote from life's realities. Ranevskaya, who herself borrows from Lopahin, gives away her last money to a drunk.

Ranevskaya's action: to stop Lopahin and offset his boorish conduct. Her upbringing does not allow her to accept such ugly behavior.

Lopahin's action: retreat. He has no intention of arguing with Ranevskaya who doesn't understand with whom she is dealing.

13. Interrupted Events

As we have noted, the same conflict may be repeated in several different events which may follow one another or be separated by other events. One should not be weary of such repetition of conflicts, thinking that a performance may become monotonous. Since the conflicts are manifested through actions, the performance dynamics are not determined mainly by the varieties of conflict but by the varieties of actions and the methods of realizing these actions.

A play may contain a number of events with the same conflict, leading and led characters, and characters' actions. It is natural to treat all these events as parts of a larger one, which we call an *interrupted* event. Thus an interrupted event is made up of several segments interspersed with other events. During our analysis of *The Cherry Orchard* we will encounter several interrupted events. One example is Event 1.17 (see page 62), which is interrupted by other events twice and each time returns to the original conflict, leading character, and actions of both sides.

14. Description of Actions

It is virtually impossible to find an exact, faithful description of action. Words are not sufficient to embody the entire diversity of psychological shades of human behavior. That is why our descriptions of action offer no more than a general idea, the basic direction in the line of behavior pursued by a character in the respective conflict. In performing the action, the actor can make it much fuller and richer, finding numerous additional shades and nuances.

Stanislavsky considered the search for a definition of the action to be an extremely important part of work on the role. In his view, as the actor searches for the verbal expression of action he penetrates ever deeper and more thoroughly into the given circumstances of the character. A process occurs of understanding and sensing the logic of the character, of understanding what is organic to his behavior. Intuition comes into play, not allowing the actor to lie and leading to authentic conflicts and actions, clarifying and, if necessary, changing them.

15. On the Monologue

Analysis of the monologue as an independent dramatic form goes beyond the scope of this book. But we cannot avoid mentioning it, as *The Cherry Orchard* has four monologues.

In this book a monologue is understood solely as the act of talking to oneself or thinking aloud—in other words, *solilo-*

quy. Through the monologue the author makes it possible for us to understand what preoccupies the character, what oppresses him, causes anxiety, invades his thoughts. Through the monologue a character reveals some of his inner world, his hidden thoughts. In this case it doesn't matter whether the character is on the stage alone or in the company of other characters. The important point is that during a monologue the character does not interact with anyone, does not seek anything from anyone. The author may set a monologue in a separate segment of the play or within an event.

As in the case of a conflict, stimulus for a monologue is invariably provided by a given circumstance or a set of given circumstances which should be presented from the point of view of the monologue speaker.

Since in the course of a monologue the character does not interact with anyone else, he is not involved in action in the sense that the term is defined in this book. Because of this there is always the danger that the monologue will lack inner development, grow lifeless, and degenerate into a static declamation in which the absence of action is masked by emotionally colored words. In order to give the monologue inner meaning and movement, it is necessary to reveal its contrasts, juxtapositions, and contradictions. The reader will find examples of such an approach to the monologue in appropriate segments of the play.

16. Summary

1. At the basis of every play is the struggle of the characters to achieve their objectives. Each character takes part in a continuous series of conflicts with other characters.

2. Conflicts do not exist ready-made in the play's story line. They are always concealed behind the author's text.

3. The parties in a conflict may be individual characters or groups of characters. One side of any conflict is the leading side, the other is the led side.

4. A conflict is based on the characters' perceptions of one another.

5. The way the characters perceive one another is determined by the given circumstances of the play. The given circumstances must always be defined from the point of view of the participants in the conflict, through their own interpretations. Only such given circumstances can give rise to conflict relations between the characters.

6. Only two types of relations are possible between the parties to a conflict. In one case the leading character imposes his view of himself on his opponent. In the other case the leading character states how he sees his opponent.

7. In the course of a conflict each character resorts to a specific tactic, or action, aimed at influencing his opponent.

8. Every play can be uniquely represented in the form of a sequence of logically independent units called events.

9. The principle of breaking a play down into events requires that each event involve only one leading character (or group of characters), which has only one conflict and one action. The event ends when the leading character ends or changes his action.

10. The framework of an event—its beginning and end—is determined by a conflict with the participation of the leading character. Besides this main conflict, an event may also include so-called incidental conflicts.

11. The leading character of the main conflict cannot participate in incidental conflicts, as this would mean the end of the event.

12. The led characters of the main conflict may be involved in incidental conflicts, during which they interrupt their actions in the main conflict of the event.

13. An interrupted event is an event broken into several segments by the intrusion of other events. All these segments have the same leading character and identical conflicts, sides, and actions.

14. A monologue is the act of talking to oneself or thinking

aloud. During a monologue the character does not interact with other characters and consequently is not involved in any conflicts.

THREE BASIC TYPES OF CONFLICTS WITHIN AN EVENT

a) A conflict between two characters (or groups of characters).

b) A conflict involving several led characters (or groups of characters) with different positions in the conflict.

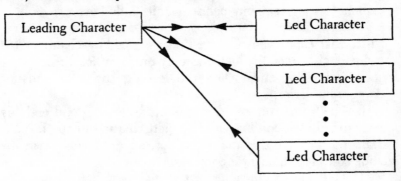

c) An incidental conflict involving a secondary character (or group of characters).

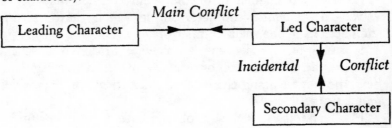

Analyzing a Play

*

It is not enough to understand and learn this method in theory, in the abstract. The method must be grasped practically, felt, become a part of oneself. The reader must learn the method by doing; the experience of performing the character's actions on the stage, as the part of the process of live interaction with partners, is essential. This goal can be achieved not only by staging the whole play but also by working on separate events and acts in a workshop environment. (A recommended selection of such events is presented in Appendix III.)

Working on a particular event, the participants must try to realize the actions of their characters while remaining within the limits of the given circumstances and the conflict of the event. But it is not advisable for actors to use the text of the play or memorize it. If an actor learns his lines right at the start, there is a danger he will be led astray. As a rule, an actor is drawn toward outward expression of the text, toward intonational coloring irrespective of the conflict. He follows the lines, the words, and, as a result, departs from the correct relationships and actions underlying the text.

In the beginning an actor is not capable of delivering the author's text naturally, because the character is still foreign to him. In the process of searching out and "feeling" for the behavior and logical thought of his character, an actor must try to find his own, approximate words which ring true and which he needs and feels at the moment.

If the character's line of behavior is found correctly and follows the logic of the author's thought, approximately the same words as those used by the author will emerge during rehearsals. Gradually the author's text becomes natural and necessary to the actor, and the approximate words are replaced with the original text.

PART TWO

Analysis of *The Cherry Orchard*

17. *Characters in the Play*

Madame RANEVSKAYA (Lyubov Andreyevna), a landowner
ANYA, her daughter, aged seventeen
VARYA, her adopted daughter, aged twenty-four
GAEV (Leonid Andreyevich), brother of Madame Ranevskaya
LOPAHIN (Yermolay Alexeyevich), a merchant
TROFIMOV (Pyotr Sergeyevich), a student
SEMYONOV-PISHCHIK, a landowner
CHARLOTTA IVANOVNA, a governess
EPIHODOV (Semyon Panteleyevich), a clerk
DUNYASHA, a maid
FIRS, an old servant, aged eighty-seven
YASHA, a young valet
The action takes place on the estate of Madame Ranevskaya.

THE LIFE OF characters does not begin with their first appearance on the stage. They come onto the stage with their pasts, and if we do not know their pasts it is impossible fully to understand and reveal their current relations and conflicts. Chekhov tells us quite a lot about the lives of his characters before the beginning of *The Cherry Orchard*. Here is a brief summary.

Lyubov Ranevskaya and her brother, Leonid Gaev, were born and brought up in the Cherry Orchard, a beautiful estate which for generations has belonged to their once rich but now impoverished family. Leonid Gaev is fifty-one years old. He is an educated and cultured nobleman who has lost his fortune without even realizing how. He is proud of his family's traditions of enlightenment and social consciousness and its contributions to the history and social development of the province. Despite his impoverished state, Gaev occupies a prominent position in local society and retains important connections: when the need arose, he readily secured for himself an excellent sinecure at a bank.

Gaev's sister, Lyubov Andreyevna Ranevskaya, is about forty-five years old (see Appendix I). Her marriage to a man "who made nothing but debts" was unsuccessful. Six years ago Ranevskaya's husband died, and she entered into an affair with a man of dubious reputation. Shortly after the start of the affair, Ranevskaya's son accidentally drowned in a river. Seeing her son's death as punishment for her sins, Ranevskaya broke up with her lover and "went away for ever, never to return, not to see that river again." But her lover followed her, then for five years lived at her expense, and finally "robbed [her] of everything and abandoned [her] for another woman." Deeply hurt and ailing after a humiliating, stupid attempt to poison herself, Ranevskaya aimlessly wiled away her days in Paris. The arrival of her daughter Anya aroused her from her despondency. It reminded her that there was a place where she was remembered and awaited, where she would find love, understanding, and sympathy—a place where she could start life anew. Ranevskaya decided to forget "that man" forever and return to Russia, to her family, to her beloved estate.

Gaev always strongly disapproved of his sister's marriage and the way of her home life. He blames her for tarnishing their family's good name and for the estrangement of their rich and influential relatives. As for Ranevskaya's last affair, he considers it too indecent even to mention it aloud. To him it simply doesn't exist.

Anya was twelve years old when Ranevskaya left for Paris. She grew up on an elegant landed estate, in an atmosphere of serene happiness, painstakingly guarded from all of life's troubles by her uncle and Varya, her adopted older sister who replaced her absent mother. The trip to Paris to visit her sick mother was Anya's first encounter with reality, with the problems and concerns of adult life hitherto unknown to her. Meeting her mother after a separation of five years, Anya viewed her through different eyes and came to know her in new ways. She is proud that she was instrumental in bringing her mother home and feels that only she really understands her.

Ranevskaya's adopted daughter, Varya, handles all the domestic and financial affairs of the home. But the mortgaged estate yields no profit, and Varya knows that it will soon be sold to pay off debts. Varya has long been in love with Lopahin, and it is commonly assumed that they will soon marry.

Lopahin is the son of a former serf of the Gaev family who has recently made a fortune. He is thirty-five to thirty-seven years old (see Appendix I). It derives from the play that Lopahin is somehow greatly indebted to Ranevskaya. In his own words, she once did so much for him that he considers her his closest and dearest friend. Gaev mentions as a self-evident fact that Lopahin can never refuse any request of Ranevskaya's, and she herself considers that she can borrow from him whenever she wishes. Chekhov does not indicate the reason for Lopahin's reverence of Ranevskaya. It would be naive to see the only reason for this in Lopahin's account of a childhood beating, when Ranevskaya soothed and comforted him. Knowing Ranevskaya's generosity and compassion, we are inclined to assume that she once helped Lopahin financially, enabling him to launch a business of his own and with time achieve his present position. It is not for nothing that he says to Ranevskaya, "Only I do want you to believe in me as you used to...."

Lopahin is quite lonely. He is attached to Ranevskaya's home, and he continued to visit it after she went abroad. The regular visits of a young bachelor to a home with a young prospective bride, Varya, has not gone unnoticed and offers food for gossip about an imminent wedding. Moreover, Lopahin himself has probably reflected about the prospect of marrying a girl from a home so dear to him. It is not accidental that Anya is so sure that Lopahin is in love with Varya.

Firs is an old, devoted servant of the Gaev family who remained with it after the liberation of the serfs—which he considers to be the cause of all current troubles and misfortunes.

Semyonov-Pishchik is a representative of an old family of nobility on the verge of losing his estate. He constantly borrows money from others.

Charlotta Ivanovna was born and grew up in a family of circus actors, but fate has turned her into a governess. She lives in the Ranevskaya house as a virtual member of the family.

The maid Dunyasha has grown up in the Ranevskaya household and is far removed from the peasant milieu from which she comes. She is seventeen to nineteen years old, and all she thinks of is admirers.

Yasha, Ranevskaya's valet, comes from peasant stock. He is about twenty-four years old. He has spent the last five years in France and realizes that he has become an entirely different person.

Epihodov, a clerk for Ranevskaya's estate, is about the same age as Yasha. He has an extremely high opinion of himself and his education. Epihodov is madly in love with Dunyasha and has proposed to her, but she hasn't yet given an answer.

Petya Trofimov is the former tutor of Ranevskaya's late son. Although already twenty-six or twenty-seven years old, he is still a student. He has been repeatedly expelled from the university for political activity. Trofimov is in love with Anya.

The events of Act I take place approximately May 6 to 10 (May 20 to 24 according to the old Russian calendar), when the cherry trees usually blossom in the southern part of central Russia (the Orel-Kursk area).

*

The four chapters that follow are devoted to an analysis of the corresponding acts of the play. The chapters are divided into sections, each of which corresponds to one event of the play and includes the text of that event, followed by a description of the given circumstances, conflicts, and actions. The sections are numbered in decimals corresponding to the number of the act and the sequential number of the event within that act. Thus 2.13 corresponds to the 13th event in Act II, and we refer to it as E2.13.

All sections are structured identically:

a. The leading character (or group of characters) is indicated in the section heading immediately after its number.

b. Text of the event.

c. Given circumstances of the leading character (as he sees them).

d. Basic conflict of the event: the leading character's position, followed by the position of the led character. In describing a conflict we shall be following a more or less uniform mode of presentation—for example, "Character X sees character Y as such-and-such a person, while character Y considers himself to be this or that." For all its literary shortcomings, this kind of notation makes it possible to set forth the relationship between the characters succinctly and unambiguously.

e. The given circumstances of the led character are set forth immediately after his position in the conflict (sometimes these circumstances are already included in his position). If there are several led characters with different positions in the conflict, we successively set forth their positions and given circumstances.

f. Actions of the characters. The action of the leading character is set forth first, followed by the actions of the led characters. Description of the action may be followed by additional notes and comments.

g. If an event includes an incidental conflict, it is described in the same sequence as the main conflict: given circumstances of the character who originates the conflict; positions of the character in the conflict; given circumstances of the opposite side; actions of the characters. If there are several incidental conflicts, they are set forth sequentially.

h. The end of each section contains directorial hints and suggestions for props, details of costumes, and small sets which may help to act this event in a workshop situation.

18. Act I

Event 1.1 (Leading Character Lopahin)

A room, which is still called the nursery. One of the doors leads to Anya's room. Dawn, sun rises during the scene. May, the cherry trees in flower but it is cold in the garden with the frost of early morning. Windows closed.

Enter Dunyasha with a candle and Lopahin with a book in his hand.

LOPAHIN: The train's in, thank God. What time is it?

DUNYASHA: Nearly two o'clock. *[Puts out the candle]* It's daylight already.

LOPAHIN: The train's late. Two hours, at least. *[Yawns and stretches]* I'm a fine one; what a fool I've been. Came here on purpose to meet them at station and fell asleep.... Dozed off as I sat in the chair. It's annoying.... You might have waked me.

DUNYASHA: I thought you had gone. *[Listens]* There, I do believe they are coming!

LOPAHIN: *[Listens]* No, what with the luggage and one thing and another.... *[A pause]*

Awakened by the sound of a passing train, Lopahin realizes that it is far past midnight and that the gentry have long since left for the station to meet Ranevskaya. Only he and the servants remain in the dark, empty house. No one roused or even thought of Lopahin, though he had come specially to meet Ranevskaya at the station. The son of a former serf, Lopahin is almost a millionaire. His style of living, new bearing, and clothes all bespeak of the great changes that have taken place with him in the years since Ranevskaya has been abroad. But what about the attitude toward him in the house! Ranevskaya's brother, Gaev, openly disregards him, publicly calling him vulgar and a money-grubber, while the maid Dunyasha, far from regarding it as her duty to wait on him, doesn't even express surprise at seeing him there. These are the circumstances which cause the conflict between Lopahin and Dunyasha.

Conflict: Lopahin views himself as a gentleman who should be treated with appropriate attention and courtesy. But Dunyasha sees no need for formality with him. He comes from the same village as she, and even though he is now rich and dresses like a gentleman, Dunyasha clearly sees the difference between Lopahin and real gentry like, say, Ranevskaya and Gaev. They were born into their position, and Lopahin bears no comparison with them.

Lopahin's action is to hammer home to Dunyasha who he is. While lamenting that he is not at the station, Lopahin stresses his closeness to Ranevskaya and his right to be there together with the other gentry. He also admonishes Dunyasha to serve him like all the others.

Dunyasha's action is to get rid of Lopahin. His talk distracts her from what is really important to her: the arrival of her mistress.

Hints: Lopahin enters wearing a vest with a heavy gold chain, a jacket slung across his arm. While speaking to Dunyasha, Lopahin unhurriedly puts on his jacket and gets himself in order. He almost does not look at Dunyasha, who is dressed up, heavily powdered and rouged, and has her hair put up.

Event 1.2 (Lopahin's Monologue)

LOPAHIN: Lyubov Andreyevna has been abroad five years; I don't know what she is like now.... She's a good person. A good-natured, kindhearted woman. I remember when I was a boy of fifteen, my late father—he used to keep a little shop here in the village in those days—gave me a punch in the face with his fist and made my nose bleed.... We were in the yard here, I forget what we'd come about—he was drunk. Lyubov Andreyevna—I can see her now—she was still young and slim then—took me to wash my face, and brought me into this very room, into the nursery. "Don't cry, little peasant," says she, "it will heal by your wedding day.".... [A pause] Little peasant.... My father was a peasant, it's true, but here I am in a white waistcoat and yellow shoes.... Like a pig in a pastry shop. Yes, I'm a rich man, but for all my money, come to think, a peasant I was, and a peasant I am.... [Turns over the pages of the book] I've been reading this book and I didn't understand a thing. It put me to sleep. [A pause]

Lopahin wraps himself in his thoughts, gradually distancing himself from Dunyasha and forgetting her presence. It is a monologue because Lopahin does not seek to communicate with Dunyasha and expects no reaction from her. Dunyasha ceases to exist for him. As noted before, for a monologue to be active it is necessary to identify juxtapositions and contrasts in it. Otherwise it becomes lifeless, either a monotonous recital or an emotional embellishment of the author's text.

The undisguised scorn with which Gaev treats Lopahin (see E1.18 and E1.30) suddenly causes him to doubt whether Ranevskaya would notice the changes that have occurred in him, whether she would accept him in his new position. After all, in the five years she has been abroad, Ranevskaya too could have changed. Recalling her, Lopahin concludes that this would be impossible: Ranevskaya had always been a person without prejudices and, unlike her brother, will not put on airs with him. But then he recalls her reference to him as

48

a "little peasant," and it makes him wonder whether she may still see him as a simple peasant. Lopahin immediately rejects the idea: he's not a peasant anymore! Yes, his father was a peasant, but he, Lopahin, is now indistinguishable from a real gentleman. But at this very moment, the book he is holding in his hand again makes him wonder whether, despite his wealth and new style of living, he is not essentially still an illiterate peasant.

Lopahin loses his confidence. He is gripped by doubts about how Ranevskaya will greet him. He is lifted from this state in turn by Dunyasha and Epihodov (in E1.3 to E1.5).

Hints: His new shoes are tight, and Lopahin is uncomfortable. From time to time Dunyasha runs up to the window glances at her pocket watch, and checks herself in the large mirror in the room.

Event 1.3 (Leading Character Dunyasha)

DUNYASHA: The dogs have been awake all night, they sense that the mistress is coming.

LOPAHIN: Why, what's the matter with you, Dunyasha....

DUNYASHA: My hands are all of a tremble. I feel as though I should faint.

LOPAHIN: You're a spoilt soft creature, Dunyasha. And dressed like a young lady, and your hair done up too. That's not the right thing. One must know one's place.

[Enter Epihodov with a bouquet; he wears a jacket and highly polished creaking top boots; he drops the bouquet as he comes in]

EPIHODOV: *[Picking up the bouquet]* Here! The gardener's sent this, says you're to put it in the dining room. *[Gives Dunyasha the bouquet]*

LOPAHIN: And bring me some kvass.

DUNYASHA: I will. *[Goes out]*

Dunyasha is so terrified over the coming meeting with her mistress that she loses control. Conflict: Dunyasha considers herself to be a genteel, frail girl incapable of coping alone

49

with the stress of expectation. Lopahin sees her as a cheeky maid who has forgotten her place. She is pestering him with ill-timed foolish talk.

Dunyasha's action is to gain an ally in Lopahin and enlist his support. Lopahin's action is to subdue Dunyasha and put her in her place. Accordingly, he gives her a dressing down and then sends her for kvass.

Note that Epihodov's appearance does not affect Lopahin's conflict with Dunyasha.

Hints: Lopahin is sitting in the armchair. He ignores Dunyasha who hangs around him, trying to get his attention.

Event 1.4 (Leading Character Epihodov)

EPIHODOV: It's chilly this morning, twenty-seven degrees, though the cherries are all in flower. I can't say much for our climate. *[Sighs]* I can't. Our climate is not often propitious to the occasion. Yermolay Alexeyevich, permit me to call your attention to the fact that I purchased myself a pair of boots the day before yesterday, and they creak, I venture to assure you, so that there's no tolerating them. What ought I to grease them with?

LOPAHIN: Leave me alone. Don't bother me.

EPIHODOV: Every day some misfortune befalls me. I don't complain, I'm used to it.... I even manage to smile. *[Dunyasha comes in, hands Lopahin the kvass]* I am going. *[Stumbles against a chair which falls over]* There.... *[As through triumphant]* There you see now, excuse the expression, an accident like that among others.... It's positively remarkable! *[Goes out]*

The clerk Epihodov is madly in love with Dunyasha. He has proposed to her and ceaselessly pursues her, seeking her consent. Today Epihodov is finely dressed in a jacket and new boots bought especially for the arrival of the mistress of the house. Knowing that the masters are all at the railway station, he has found a suitable pretext to come into the house and show off in front of Dunyasha. Dunyasha, however, has been sent off, and Epihodov unexpectedly finds himself alone with Lopahin, who pays not the slightest attention to him.

Conflict: Epihodov considers himself to be a cultured, educated person quite worthy of having conversation with such an important person as Lopahin. To Lopahin he is a man who has forgotten his place. He keeps pestering Lopahin with stupid talk, even going so far as to ask how to grease his boots!

Epihodov's action is to impress Lopahin. Lopahin's action is to put Epihodov in his place.

Hints: Lopahin is sitting down. Epihodov importantly, like a guest, strolls across the room, frequently glancing at himself in the mirror. A chair that can be easily upturned is necessary for this scene (the rest of the furniture in the room, in general, is heavy and sturdy). Dunyasha brings in a large mug of kvass, but Lopahin is not drinking it.

Event 1.5 (Leading Character Dunyasha)

DUNYASHA: Do you know, Yermolay Alexeyevich, I must confess, Epihodov has made me a proposal.

LOPAHIN: Ah!

DUNYASHA: I'm sure I don't know.... He's a harmless fellow, but sometimes when he begins talking, there's no making anything of it. It's all very fine and expressive, only incomprehensible. I sort of like him too. He loves me to distraction. He's an unlucky man; every day there's something. They tease him about it—two-and-twenty-misfortunes they call him.

LOPAHIN: *[Listening]* There! I do believe they're coming....

DUNYASHA: They are coming! What's the matter with me?... I'm cold all over.

LOPAHIN: They really are coming. Let's go and meet them. Will she recognize me? It's been five years since we've seen each other.

DUNYASHA: *[In an agitation]* I shall faint this very second.... Ah, I'll faint!

[There is a sound of two carriages driving up to the house. Lopahin and Dunyasha go out quickly. The stage is left empty.]

Lopahin has piqued Dunyasha by disparaging what she is most proud of: her self-image as a young lady. The conflict is similar to that in E1.3: Dunyasha sees herself as a dainty, sensitive girl, virtually a real young lady, while to Lopahin she is no more than a cheeky maid who has forgotten her station. The characters' actions, however, differ. Dunyasha's action is to defend herself and emphasize her difference from a simple rustic maid. She is madly loved by such an educated and cultured person as Epihodov, though she doubts whether he is good enough for her. Furthermore, when she becomes agitated Dunyasha is unable to control her weak nerves and is ready to swoon, like a real lady. Lopahin's action is to avoid getting into a conversation with Dunyasha and to direct her attention toward the imminent arrival of Ranevskaya.

It should be noted that the relations between the characters in E1.1 and E1.3 to E1.5 are similar in that the servants fail to realize the distance separating them from Lopahin. What they do see is the great difference between Lopahin and the real gentry. To the servants he remains a person who, like them, comes from peasant stock. That the servants are not sufficiently deferential toward him increases Lopahin's doubts as to whether Ranevskaya will recognize him.

Hints: Dunyasha speaks about Epihodov's proposal as it were something funny and not quite suitable for her. Lopahin paces the room listening attentively to the sounds from outside.

Event 1.6 (Leading Characters Anya and Varya)

[A noise is heard in the adjoining rooms. Firs, who has driven to meet Ranevskaya, crosses the stage hurriedly, leaning on a cane. He is wearing old-fashioned livery and a high hat. He is talking to himself, but not a word can be

distinguished. A voice: "Come, let's go in here." Enter Lyubov Andreyevna, Anya, and Charlotta Ivanovna with a pet dog on a leash, all in traveling dresses. Varya, in an overcoat with a kerchief over her head, Gaev, Semyonov-Pishchik, Lopahin, Dunyasha with bag and umbrella, servants with other articles. All walk across the room]

ANYA: Let's come in here. Do you remember what room this is, mamma?

RANEVSKAYA: *[Joyfully, through her tears]* The nursery!

VARYA: How cold it is, my hands are numb. *[To Lyubov]* Your rooms, the white room and the lavender one, are just the same as ever, mamma.

RANEVSKAYA: My nursery, dear delightful room.... I used to sleep here when I was little.... *[Cries]* And here I am, like a little child again.... *[Kisses her brother and Varya, and then her brother again]* Varya's just the same as ever, like a nun. And I recognized Dunyasha.... *[Kisses Dunyasha]*

The leading side in this event is a group consisting of Anya and Varya.

Five years ago Ranevskaya left her home and immersed herself in a different life. Today she has finally returned to her family. Conflict: Ranevskaya's daughters see her as estranged from her family, as having forgotten everything here and having other concerns and interests. Ranevskaya, for her part, has always been and remains a part of this world and cannot conceive of life outside it. Now, when she has parted with her lover, she can at last return to her family.

The action of the group is to reintroduce Ranevskaya to the life of the house and the family. Ranevskaya's action is to gather around herself all the people dear and close to her and prove her love and devotion.

Hints: While Ranevskaya was away, the room was remodeled. Anya stops Ranevskaya and, together with Varya and Gaev, watches with a great interest to see whether Ranevskaya recognizes her nursery.

Event 1.7 (Leading Character Gaev)

> GAEV: The train was two hours late. What do you think of that? Is that the way to do things?
> CHARLOTTA: *[To Pishchik]* My dog eats nuts, too.
> PISHCHIK: *[Wonderingly]* Fancy that!
> *[They all go out except Anya and Dunyasha]*

Today the household is engrossed in one great event: Ranevskaya's return. Conflict: Gaev thinks that Charlotta, like the others, is also caught up in this exciting event. But Charlotta has her own small joys and interests. She has not seen the courteous Mr. Pishchik for some time and wouldn't mind talking to him. Gaev's action is to get Charlotta to join the family rejoicing. Charlotta's action is to stay apart. The sociable Pishchik feels he cannot leave her alone.

Hints: Charlotta and Pishchik are slightly distant to the others. Charlotta has a dog in her arms (a stuffed dog may be used).

Event 1.8 (Leading Character Dunyasha)

> DUNYASHA: We've been expecting you so long.... *[Takes Anya's hat and coat]*
> ANYA: I haven't slept for four nights on the trip.... I feel dreadfully cold.
> DUNYASHA: You set out in Lent, there was snow and frost, and now? My darling! *[Laughs and kisses her]* I have missed you, my precious, my joy.... I must tell you at once, I can't put off a minute....
> ANYA: *[Wearily]* Again something....
> DUNYASHA: The clerk, Epihodov, proposed to me just after Easter.
> ANYA: It's always the same subject with you.... *[Fixing her hair]* I've lost all my hairpins. *[She is staggering from exhaustion]*
> DUNYASHA: I don't know what to think, really. He does love me, he does love me so!
> ANYA: *[Looking toward her door, tenderly]* My own room,

my windows just as though I had never gone away. I'm home! Tomorrow morning I shall get up and run into the garden.... Oh, if I could get to sleep! I haven't slept all the journey, I was so anxious and worried.

DUNYASHA: Pyotr Sergeyevich came the day before yesterday.

ANYA: *[Joyfully]* Petya!

DUNYASHA: He sleeps in the bath house, he has settled in there. I'm afraid to be a bother, says he. *[Glancing at her watch]* I was to have waked him, but Varvara Michailovna told me not to. Don't wake him, says she.

[Enter Varya with a bunch of keys at her waist]

VARYA: Dunyasha, coffee and make haste.... Mamma's asking for coffee.

DUNYASHA: This very minute. *[Goes out]*

This event was examined in greater detail in Part I. Dunyasha is delighted with the return of Anya, whom she has missed so much. At last there is a person with whom she can share her news, secrets, and gossip.

Conflict: Dunyasha sees Anya as a friend rather than a mistress. But Anya, brimming with new impressions and concerns, finds nothing in common with the maid Dunyasha.

Dunyasha's action is to get Anya's attention and arouse her interest. Anya's action is to distance herself from Dunyasha.

Hints: A sofa with cushions and a blanket are necessary for this scene.

Event 1.9 (Leading Character Anya)

VARYA: Well, thank God, you've come. You're home again. My little darling has come back! My precious beauty has come back again!

ANYA: I have had a time of it!

VARYA: I can imagine!

ANYA: We set off in Holy Week—it was so cold then. All the way Charlotta talked and showed off her tricks. What did you burden me with Charlotta for?

VARYA: You couldn't have traveled all alone, darling. At seventeen!

ANYA: We got to Paris at last, it was cold there, snow. I speak French terribly. Mamma lives on the fifth floor, I went up to her and there were some Frenchmen, ladies, an old priest with a book. The place smelt of tobacco and was so uncomfortable. Suddenly I felt sorry for mamma, so sorry. I put my arms round her neck, and hugged her and wouldn't let her go. Mamma was as kind as she could be, and she cried....

VARYA: *[Through her tears]* Don't say any more, don't say....

ANYA: She had sold her villa at Menton, she had nothing left, nothing. I hadn't a penny left either, we only had just enough to get here. And mamma doesn't understand! When we had dinner at the stations, she always ordered the most expensive things and tipped the waiters a whole ruble. Charlotta's just the same. Yasha too must have the same as we do; it's simply awful. You know Yasha is mamma's valet, we brought him here with us.

VARYA: I saw the scoundrel.

ANYA: Well, has the interest on the mortgage been paid?

VARYA: Good heavens, no.

ANYA: Oh dear, oh dear....

VARYA: In August the estate will be sold....

ANYA: Oh dear....

Anya's trip to Paris has brought her for the first time in touch with life's concerns and difficulties, with the hitherto unknown world of adults. She has also rediscovered her mother whom she grew up without. Anya realizes that her mother is ill adapted to life and needs help and support.

Conflict: Anya sees herself as an adult, capable of taking part in all family affairs, but to Varya she is still a child. Anya's action is to draw Varya into a discussion of family affairs. Varya's action is to avoid any kind of discussion, so she makes do with superficial remarks.

Hints: Varya hugs Anya, caringly looks her over, notices an expensive brooch. Anya, checking the doorway to ensure not being overheard, is hurrying to tell Varya something very important.

Event 1.10 (Leading Character Anya)

LOPAHIN: *[Poking his head in at the door, bleats]* Mah-h-h. ... *[Disappears]*

VARYA: *[Weeping]* There, that's what I could do to him.... *[Shakes her fist]*

ANYA: *[Embracing Varya, softly]* Varya, has he proposed to you? *[Varya shakes her head]* Why, but he loves you.... Why is it you don't come to an understanding? What are you waiting for?

VARYA: I believe that there never will be anything between us. He has a lot to do, he has no time for me...and takes no notice of me. Good riddance, it makes me miserable to see him.... Everyone's talking about our wedding, everyone's congratulating me, and all the while there's really nothing in it; it's all like a dream.... *[In another tone]* You have a brooch like a bee.

ANYA: *[Mournfully]* Mamma bought it. *[Goes into her own room and in a lighthearted, childish tone]* And you know, in Paris I went up in a balloon!

Varya's angry reaction to a joke by Lopahin, whom she intends to marry, indicates that not all is smooth in their relations. The conflict here is the same as in the previous event: Anya sees herself as an adult member of the family, capable of taking part in all its affairs, while to Varya she is still a child. Anya is unable to understand the complexities of the relationship between Varya and Lopahin. Anya's action is to teach, direct, and stimulate an inactive Varya. Varya's action is to put an end to talk about marriage.

Hints: Anya hugs Varya, thus inviting her to have an intimate conversation. Varya, on the other hand, starts picking up Anya's scattered things and shifts the conversation to the brooch.

Event 1.11 (Leading Character Varya)

VARYA: My darling's home again! My beauty is home again!

[*Dunyasha returns with a coffeepot and is making the coffee*]

VARYA: [*Standing at the door*] All day long, darling, as I go about looking after the house, I keep dreaming all the time. If only we could marry you to a rich man, then I should feel more at rest. Then I would go off to a monastery, then to Kiev...to Moscow, and so I would go from one holy place to another.... I would go on and on. Heavenly!...

ANYA: The birds are singing in the garden. What time is it?

VARYA: It must be nearly three. It's time you were asleep, darling. [*Going into Anya's room*] Heavenly!

At last Anya leaves behind all unpleasantness and regains her usual serenity of a happy child. Conflict: Varya regards herself inseparable from Anya and responsible for her life. But Anya sees Varya as a rather narrow-minded person incapable of understanding Anya or her interests. Varya has some stupid plans about Anya's future which are based on her primitive notions of life. Note that Anya's views have been influenced by Trofimov, who usually spends the summer at the Ranevskaya estate.

Varya's action is to bring Anya into her plans and thoughts. She has no one closer than Anya. Anya's action is to distance herself.

Hints: Standing in the doorway, Varya looks admiringly at Anya, who is twirling happily in her room and then turns toward the window and interrupts Varya's discourse. Dunyasha is next to a table set for coffee.

Event 1.12 (Leading Character Dunyasha)

[*Yasha enters with a rug and a traveling bag*]

YASHA: [*Crosses the stage, mincingly*] May one come in here, pray?

DUNYASHA: I wouldn't have recognized you, Yasha. How you have changed abroad.

YASHA: H'm!... And who are you?

DUNYASHA: When you went away, I was that high.... *[Shows distance from the floor]* Dunyasha, Fyodor Kozodoev's daughter. You don't remember me!

YASHA: H'm!... You're a peach! *[Looks round and embraces her; she shrieks and drops a saucer. Yasha goes out hastily]*

This event was examined in greater detail in Part I. In the years since Ranevskaya has been away, Dunyasha has blossomed and become quite a young lady. She enjoys tremendous success among the local young men and has no doubt that she is irresistible. The clerk Epihodov, an educated and courteous young man, follows her about, begging her to marry him. Dunyasha, however, refuses to give him an answer, because she is not sure whether he is good enough for her. When Dunyasha sees the valet Yasha, she is struck by his foreign looks and mannerisms.

Conflict: Dunyasha sees Yasha as a suitable mate, an embodiment of her dreams. But "Europeanized" Yasha feels he can have nothing in common with a simple rustic maid. Living in Paris for five years has changed him completely. He no longer belongs to the provincial life nor to simple, ignorant folk.

Dunyasha's action is to arouse Yasha's interest in her. Yasha's action is to emphasize the distance between them. First he refuses to recognize her, then, in response to her playful small talk, he condescends to Dunyasha and unceremoniously embraces her.

Hints: Yasha, peering at Dunyasha, presses his advance. Dunyasha does not step back, allowing Yasha to admire her.

Event 1.13 (Leading Character Varya)

VARYA: *[In the doorway, in a tone of vexation]* What's going on here?

DUNYASHA: *[Through her tears]* I have broken a saucer....
VARYA: Well, that brings good luck.

Dunyasha has done something wrong again. Conflict: Varya sees herself as being responsible for everything that occurs in the house. Dunyasha thinks Varya is assuming too much control and intervening in things that do not concern her. Varya's action is to bring Dunyasha to heel. Dunyasha's action is to lull Varya's vigilance. She has no intention of letting her in on her personal affairs.

Hints: Varya quickly checks the room, ensuring that everything is in order. Dunyasha, forcing tears, looks directly into Varya's eyes.

Event 1.14 (Leading Character Anya)

ANYA: *[Coming out of her room]* We ought to prepare mamma: Petya is here....
VARYA: I told them not to wake him.
ANYA: *[Pensively]* Six years ago father died, and a month later little brother Grisha was drowned in the river, such a beautiful boy he was, only seven. It was more than mamma could bear, and she went away, went away without looking back.... *[Shuddering]* How well I understand her, if only she knew! *[A pause]* And Petya was Grisha's tutor, he may remind her....

Anya is reminded of Trofimov's arrival and recalls the drama that occurred in their family. This is a repetition of the conflict in E1.9 and E1.10: Anya sees herself as a mature person capable of participating in all the family's affairs. But to Varya she is still a child. Neither Varya nor Gaev (see E1.40) wishes to discuss the personal affairs of Anya's mother with her. Anya's action is to draw Varya into a discussion of her mother. Varya's action is to avoid this.

Hints: While speaking about her mother, Anya stops from time to time, waiting for Varya's reaction. Varya is overseeing the cleanup, pointing out to Dunyasha pieces of the saucer which she has failed to pick up.

Event 1.15 (Leading Character Firs)

> *[Enter Firs, wearing a jacket and a white waistcoat]*
> FIRS: *[Goes up to the coffee pot, anxiously]* The mistress
> will be served here.... *[Puts on white gloves]* Is the coffee
> ready? *[Sternly to Dunyasha]* Girl! Where's the cream?
> DUNYASHA: Ah, goodness me! *[Goes out quickly]*
> FIRS: *[Fussing round the coffee pot]* Ech! you good-for-
> nothing.... *[Muttering to himself]* Come back from Paris....
> And the old master used to go to Paris, too...by horses....
> *[Laughs]*

At last the mistress of the house has returned. Now life will
revert to its old patterns, which no one but Firs remembers.

Conflict: Firs sees himself as the only and irreplaceable
person in the house whom all the servants must look up to.
But to Dunyasha he is a bothersome old man who intrudes
upon her at the most unsuitable time. Right now she is
wrapped in romantic dreams. Firs's action is to give Dunyasha a lesson and to set an example. Dunyasha's action is to
avoid conversation with Firs. Even now she is not listening to
what he is saying.

Hints: Firs puts his cane in the corner upon entering the
room. He emphatically holds himself erect. Dunyasha gladly
leaves Firs.

Event 1.16 (Leading Character Varya)

> VARYA: What is it, Firs?
> FIRS: What is your pleasure? *[Gleefully]* My lady has
> come home! I have lived to see her again! Now I can
> die.... *[Cries from happiness]*

Old Firs is deteriorating; again he mumbles something to
himself. Conflict: To Varya, Firs is a frail old man who needs
help and supervision. But Firs has revived to a new life. After
many years of obscurity, his life is again filled with meaning—
everyone needs him, he is back at his post. At last! Varya's action is to keep an eye on Firs. Firs's action is to explain and

impress upon Varya the huge change that has taken place in the life of the house.

Hints: In answer to Firs's mumbling, Varya comes and hands him his cane. Firs ignores the cane.

Event 1.17 (Leading Character Ranevskaya)

[Enter Lyubov Andreyevna, Gaev, and Semyonov-Pishchik. Gaev, as he comes in, makes a gesture with his arms and his whole body, as though he were playing billiards]

RANEVSKAYA: How does it go? Let me remember.... Yellow in the corner; double shot to the middle!

GAEV: That's it—cut into the corner! Why, once, sister, we used to sleep together in this very room, and now I'm fifty-one, strange as it seems....

This is a conflict between Ranevskaya and Gaev. It is an *interrupted* event consisting of three parts interspaced by Events E1.18–E1.19 and E1.20–E1.21.

After the tragedy of breaking with her lover, after all her troubles, suffering, and humiliation (see E2.6), Ranevskaya is once again with her family, in her beloved house which she has missed so much all these years. And even though Ranevskaya has already been told that the estate is up for sale (see E1.22), she doesn't want to think about it or discuss it; she simply refuses to dampen the joy of the reunion.

Conflict: Ranevskaya feels happy and reinvigorated; her life is starting anew. Gaev, on the other hand, thinks his sister is out of touch with reality and doesn't realize the hopelessness of their situation. Gaev already knows that Ranevskaya has returned with no money, and thus their last hope of salvation has collapsed.

Action: Ranevskaya's action is to gather all her friends and relatives together so they can join in the joy and merriment of reunion. Gaev's action is to make his sister face reality. He does not share Ranevskaya's delight and turns the conversation to the sad changes that have taken place.

Hints: Ranevskaya is wearing an elegant Parisian outfit. She pleasurably repeats forgotten billiard terminology. Lopahin constantly tries to be in her view.

Event 1.18 (Leading Character Gaev)

> LOPAHIN: Yes, time flies.
> GAEV: What?
> LOPAHIN: Time, I say, flies.
> GAEV: What a smell of patchouli!

Lopahin unceremoniously intervenes in a family conversation. Conflict: To Gaev, Lopahin is a person who has no place in their house. But Lopahin considers himself a close and equal member of the group, like Gaev and Pishchik. Ranevskaya has greeted Lopahin with sincere warmth, and all his fears have been dispelled (see E1.2, E1.5).

Gaev's action is to reject Lopahin, making him understand he is a stranger and an undesirable. Lopahin's action is to stand up for himself and his right to be there.

Hints: Gaev speaks into space, looking past Lopahin.

Event 1.19 (Leading Character Anya)

> ANYA: I'm going to bed. Good night, mamma. *[Kisses her mother]*
> RANEVSKAYA: My precious darling. *[Kisses her hands]* Are you glad to be home? I can't believe it.
> ANYA: Goodbye, uncle.
> GAEV: *[Kisses her face and hands]* God bless you! How like you are to your mother! *[To his sister]* At her age you were just the same, Lyuba.
> *[Anya shakes hands with Lopahin and Pishchik, then goes out, shutting the door after her]*
> RANEVSKAYA: She's quite worn out.
> PISHCHIK: Yes, it's a long trip, to be sure.

Conflict between Anya and Gaev. Today, the day of mother's arrival, uncle has again had a confrontation with Lopahin.

Conflict: Anya thinks herself sufficiently grown up to voice her own opinion in the family. But to Gaev she is a child incapable of understanding his relations with Lopahin. There is no place for Lopahin in this house, and Gaev never loses an opportunity to demonstrate this.

Anya's action is to stop the unpleasant scene by suddenly leaving. She displays her pique by refusing to kiss her uncle as she leaves. Gaev's action is to soothe and distract Anya, pretending that nothing has happened. Ranevskaya, under the impressions of her reunion with the family and the home, ignores the incident, attributing Anya's sudden departure to fatigue.

Hints: Anya loudly announces her departure and purposely does not look at her uncle.

Event 1.20 (Leading Character Varya)

VARYA: *[To Lopahin and Pishchik]* Well, gentlemen? It's three o'clock and time to say goodbye.

RANEVSKAYA: *[Laughs]* You're just the same as ever, Varya. *[Draws her to her and kisses her]* I'll just drink my coffee and then we will all go and rest. *[Firs puts a cushion under her feet]* Thanks, dear friend. I am so fond of coffee, I drink it day and night. Thanks, my dear old man. *[Kisses Firs]*

VARYA: I'll just see whether all the things have been brought in.... *[Goes out]*

The guests have clearly outstayed their welcome. They have greeted Ranevskaya, and now it is time to leave her with her family whom she has not seen for five years.

The conflict is between Varya and Ranevskaya and a group comprising Pishchik and Lopahin. Varya views herself as the mistress responsible for everything going on in the house. To Ranevskaya, Varya is a person who cannot spend a minute without doing something (see Ranevskaya's opinion of Varya in E2.7 and E4.14). Even today she can't relax. Pishchik and Lopahin, for their part, consider Varya too presumptuous—the mistress of the house is Ranevskaya, and she knows what to do.

Varya's action is to keep all domestic affairs under her control. Ranevskaya's action is to keep Varya close. Today she wants to be with her family. Lopahin and Pishchik ignore Varya's words.

Hints: Ranevskaya embraces Varya and tries to seat her next to herself.

Event 1.17 (continued)

RANEVSKAYA: Can it really be me sitting here? *[Laughs]* I want to dance about and clap my hands. *[Covers her face with her hands]* What if I'm just dreaming! God knows I love my country, I love it dearly; I couldn't look out the window in the train, I kept crying so. *[Through her tears]* But I must drink my coffee, though. Thank you, Firs, dear old man. I'm so glad to see you're still alive.

FIRS: The day before yesterday.

GAEV: He's rather deaf.

Event 1.21 (Leading Characters Lopahin and Pishchik)

LOPAHIN: I have to set off for Kharkov right away, at five o'clock.... It is annoying! I wanted just to look at you, and have a little talk.... You are just as splendid as ever.

PISHCHIK: *[Breathing heavily]* Even prettier.... Dressed in Parisian style...completely bowled me over.

LOPAHIN: Your brother, Leonid Andreyevich here, says everywhere that I'm vulgar, that I'm a money-grabber, but I don't care one straw for that. Let him talk. Only I do want you to believe in me as you used to. I do want your wonderful eyes to look at me as they used to in the old days. Merciful God! My father was a serf of your father and of your grandfather, but you—you—did so much for me once, that I've forgotten all that; I love you as though you were my family...more than my family.

Conflict between Ranevskaya and a group comprising Lopahin and Pishchik. Despite the late hour and Varya's attempt to get rid of them, Ranevskaya lets Lopahin and Pishchik stay on.

Conflict: Lopahin and Pishchik regard themselves as friends of the family whom Ranevskaya is happy to see in her house. But today they are uninvited guests, intruders, keeping her from meeting with her household and family.

Lopahin's and Pishchik's action is to gain Ranevskaya's attention. Ranevskaya's action is to ignore them. Today she has no need for anyone except her family.

Hints: Lopahin and Pishchik are vying with each other for Ranevskaya's attention. Ranevskaya looks around the room noticing neither of them.

Event 1.17 (continued)

RANEVSKAYA: I can't sit still, I simply can't.... *[Jumps up and walks about in violent agitation]* This happiness is too much for me.... You may laugh at me, I know I'm silly.... My dear little bookcase.... *[Kisses the bookcase]* My little table.

GAEV: Our nurse died while you were away.

RANEVSKAYA: *[Sits down and drinks coffee]* Yes, the Kingdom of Heaven be hers. They wrote me.

GAEV: And Anastasy is dead. Cross-eyed Petrushka has left me and is in service now with the police captain in the town. *[Takes a box of caramels out of his pocket and sucks one]*

PISHCHIK: My daughter, Dashenka, sends her love to you.

Event 1.22 (Leading Character Lopahin)

LOPAHIN: I want to tell you something very pleasant and cheering. *[Glancing at his watch]* I'm going right away...there's no time to say much...well, I can say it in a couple of words. Now you know that your cherry orchard is to be sold to pay your debts; the twenty-second of August is the day fixed for the sale; but don't worry, dearest lady, you may sleep in peace, there is a way of saving it.... This is what I propose. I beg your attention! Your estate is not thirteen miles from the town, the railway runs close by it, and if the cherry orchard and the land along the river bank were cut into building plots and then let on lease for summer cottages, you would make an income of at least twenty-five thousand rubles a year out of it.

GAEV: That's a lot of nonsense, if you'll excuse me.

RANEVSKAYA: I don't quite understand you, Yermolay Alexeyevich.

LOPAHIN: You will get a rent of at least twenty-five rubles a year for a three-acre plot from summer residents, and if you say the word now, I'll bet you what you like there won't be one square foot of ground vacant by the autumn, all the plots will be taken up. I congratulate you; in fact, you are saved. It's a perfect location with the deep river. Only, of course, it must be cleared—all the old buildings, for example, must be removed, this house too, which is really good for nothing, and the old cherry orchard must be cut down....

RANEVSKAYA: Cut down? My dear fellow, forgive me, but you don't know what you are talking about. If there is one thing interesting—remarkable indeed—in the whole province, it's just our cherry orchard.

LOPAHIN: The only thing remarkable about the orchard is that it's a very large one. There's a crop of cherries every alternate year, and then there's nothing to be done with them, no one buys them.

GAEV: And this orchard is mentioned in the Encyclopedia.

LOPAHIN: [*Glancing at his watch*] If we don't decide on something and don't take some steps, on the twenty-second of August the cherry orchard and the whole estate too will be sold by auction. Make up your minds! There is no other way of saving it, I'll swear to that. Absolutely!

FIRS: In old days, forty or fifty years ago, they used to dry the cherries, soak them, pickle them, make jam too, and they used...

GAEV: Be quiet, Firs.

FIRS: And they used to send the preserved cherries to Moscow and to Kharkov by the wagonload. That brought

67

the money in! And the preserved cherries in those days were soft and juicy, sweet and fragrant...they knew the way to do them then....

RANEVSKAYA: And where is the recipe now?

FIRS: It's forgotten. Nobody remembers it.

PISHCHIK: *[To Lyubov Andreyevna]* What's it like in Paris? Did you eat frogs?

RANEVSKAYA: I ate crocodiles.

PISHCHIK: Fancy that now!...

LOPAHIN: There used to be only the landowners and the peasants in the country, but now there are these summer residents. All the towns, even the small ones, are surrounded nowadays by summer cottages. And one may say for sure, that in another twenty years there will be many more of these people and they'll be everywhere. At present the summer resident only drinks tea on his verandah, but maybe he'll take to working his bit of land too, and then your cherry orchard would become happy, rich and prosperous....

GAEV: *[Indignant]* What nonsense!

Lopahin has hit on a great idea for saving Ranevskaya from imminent ruin, and he knows his plan is unassailable. Finally he can repay Ranevskaya for her kindness, for all she has done for him.

The conflict is between Lopahin and a group consisting of Ranevskaya, Gaev, and Firs. Lopahin sees himself as the savior of Ranevskaya's family, someone who knows exactly what they must do in this modern life. But they see him as a stranger who has forgotten his place and is interfering in affairs that don't concern him. Lopahin is basically incapable of understanding their life or values. To Gaev and Ranevskaya there is nothing more dear than their family estate, and the very idea of destroying what had for generations been the glory and pride of their family is sacrilege. To Firs, too, life is inseparable from the Gaev family and their estate. He is the last bearer of old traditions.

Lopahin's action is utterly to surprise, to startle. His opponents' action is to put him in his place. He has forgotten who he is, and is trying to judge things which are beyond his comprehension. Gaev and Ranevskaya immediately interrupt him while Firs comes to the defense of the orchard (i.e., the old way of life), going on to explain that it is not the orchard that has changed but people, who have forgotten all the good old things.

In this event there is also an incidental conflict between Pishchik and Ranevskaya in which Pishchik is the leading character. Lopahin has broached the unpleasant topic of the estate at an inappropriate time, spoiling Ranevskaya's festive mood. Pishchik rushes in to salvage the situation. Conflict: Pishchik sees himself as a man of the world who knows what to say and when to say it. But to Ranevskaya he is rather eccentric and prone to odd behavior. He starts talking about her Paris life—which is a painful topic for her.

Pishchik's action is to distract Ranevskaya. He has no doubt that she will be delighted to talk about her gay life in Paris. Ranevskaya's action is to cut Pishchik out.

Hints: Lopahin walks out into the middle of the room and solemnly announces his project. At first Ranevskaya tries to understand what the conversation is about, and then loses all interest in what Lopahin says.

Event 1.23 (Leading Character Ranevskaya)

[Enter Varya and Yasha]

VARYA: There are two telegrams for you, mamma. *[Takes out keys and opens an old-fashioned bookcase with a loud crack]* Here they are.

RANEVSKAYA: They're from Paris. *[Tears up the telegrams without reading them]* I have done with Paris....

GAEV: Do you know, Lyuba, how old that bookcase is? Last week I pulled out the bottom drawer and there I found the date branded on it. The bookcase was made just a hundred years ago. What do you say to that? We might have celebrated its jubilee. Though it's an inanimate object, still it is a bookcase.

69

PISHCHIK: *[Amazed]* A hundred years.... Fancy that now!

Varya is in a hurry to give Ranevskaya telegrams from her former lover. Varya and Gaev are still unaware that the telegrams mean nothing to Ranevskaya, that she has irrevocably broken with the man and returned to her family for good.

The conflict is between Ranevskaya and the members of her family, Gaev and Varya. Ranevskaya sees them as impatient to hear the details of her personal life. But Gaev considers it below his dignity to be involved in her scandalous private affairs. He denounces his sister's morals and style of living (see E1.39), and wants to hear nothing about her lover. Besides, Ranevskaya has clearly forgotten herself and made these references in the presence of strangers and Varya. Varya, for her part, considers it inappropriate to discuss her adoptive mother's personal life.

Ranevskaya's action is to familiarize everyone with the details of her life. The past is done with, and she has returned to her family for good. Gaev's action is to interrupt Ranevskaya and distract her from an unsavory topic. He achieves this by changing the subject of the conversation to a discourse about a hundred-year-old bookcase, which turns into a speech addressed to the bookcase.

Hints: Gaev makes a point of not seeing the telegrams or hearing Ranevskaya.

Event 1.24 (Gaev's Monologue)

GAEV: Yes.... It is a thing.... *[Feeling the bookcase]* Dear, honored, bookcase! Hail to thee who for more than a hundred years hast served the pure ideals of good and justice; thy silent call to fruitful labor has never flagged in those hundred years, maintaining *[in tears]* in generations of our family, courage and faith in a brighter future and fostering in us ideals of good and social consciousness. *[A pause]*

This is a monologue; Gaev neither tries to communicate with other characters nor seeks anything from them. The motivation for the monologue is Lopahin's suggestion to tear down the house and cut down the fine orchard. Gaev is especially indignant over the suggestion that vacationers may some day replace his family. To Gaev the hundred-year-old bookcase is an embodiment of the honor and pride of his ancient family, of the beautiful old way of life with its culture, spiritual values, and moral humanism. None of this is of any value to Lopahin and his sort. In their view anything without direct gain is obsolete, useless, and should be destroyed.

In his monologue Gaev counterposes the lack of spirituality in modern life with his faith in the stability of noble old principles, in the spirit of which his forebears were reared. He refuses to believe all their efforts were in vain and all they created may disappear, overrun by barbarians and money-grubbers. Gaev's monologue involuntarily reflects the matters that oppress him: despair caused by the imminent loss of the estate, and a sense of helplessness to do anything about it.

Hints: Gaev turns to his dear books which are kept in the bookcase.

Event 1.25 (Leading Character Lopahin)

LOPAHIN: Yes....
RANEVSKAYA: You are just the same as ever, Leonid.
GAEV: [*A little embarrassed*] Bank off the corner into the side pocket!
LOPAHIN: [*Looking at his watch*] Well, I've got to go.

Lopahin must leave soon, but Ranevskaya, instead of discussing business and thinking about his plan, listens to Gaev's meaningless chatter. Conflict: Lopahin sees himself as the only sensible person in the gathering, worthy of attention. But to Ranevskaya and Gaev he is a stranger, out of place in their world. Gaev is talking about things close and understandable to them alone.

Lopahin's action is to draw attention to himself and get down to a businesslike conversation. Ranevskaya's and Gaev's action is to distance themselves from Lopahin. At the same time Gaev is rather embarrassed for having given voice to his innermost feelings in the presence of Lopahin who can never understand them.

Hints: Lopahin does not even attempt to leave, though he checks his watch. Moved, Ranevskaya comes up to her brother.

Event 1.26 (Leading Character Pishchik)

YASHA: *[Handing Lyubov Andreyevna medicine]* Perhaps you will take your pills now....

PISHCHIK: You shouldn't take medicines, my dear madam...they do no harm and no good.... Give them here...honored lady. *[Takes the pillbox, pours the pills into the palm of his hand, blows on them, puts them in his mouth, and drinks off some kvass]* There!

RANEVSKAYA: *[In alarm]* Why, you must be out of your mind!

PISHCHIK: I have taken all the pills.

LOPAHIN: What a glutton! *[All laugh]*

FIRS: His honor stayed with us at Easter, ate half a bucket of pickles.... *[Mutters]*

RANEVSKAYA: What is he saying?

VARYA: He has taken to muttering like that for the last three years. We are used to it.

YASHA: Advanced age.

No one understands how to greet a glamorous lady like Ranevskaya. First Gaev and Lopahin have a spat, then Lopahin reminds her of the troubles with the estate, and to cap it all Gaev starts babbling and moves himself to tears. All that is left for Ranevskaya is to swallow her pills and retire.

Conflict between Pishchik and Ranevskaya: Pishchik sees himself as a person capable of cheering up and entertaining the company. But to Ranevskaya he is an eccentric who frightens people with his wild antics. One can never expect anything reasonable of Pishchik.

Pishchik's action is to keep Ranevskaya from leaving and

thus prolong the party. Ranevskaya's action is to stop Pishchik and make him stop his dangerous jokes. She is joined by Firs, who tells of another antic by Pishchik.

Hints: Pishchik imitates a magician. He washes down the pills with the kvass which was brought by Dunyasha in E1.4.

Event 1.27 (Leading Character Lopahin)

[*Charlotta Ivanovna, a very thin, lean figure in a white dress with a lorgnette in her belt, walks across the stage*]
LOPAHIN: I beg your pardon, Charlotta Ivanovna, I have not had time to greet you. [*Tries to kiss her hand*]
CHARLOTTA: [*Pulling away her hand*] If I let you kiss my hand, you'll next be wanting to kiss my elbow, and then my shoulder....
LOPAHIN: I've no luck today! [*All laugh*]

Seeing Charlotta pass by, Lopahin realizes that he has committed a faux pas by failing to greet her. Conflict: Lopahin sees himself as a man of society, a real gentleman. But Charlotta thinks he is behaving ridiculously and out of character. She is not yet used to Lopahin's new manners.

Lopahin's action is to show himself off. Ranevskaya hasn't yet realized what he has become and the change he has undergone. Charlotta's action is to make fun of Lopahin.

Hints: Charlotta covers her shoulders and arms with a shawl, as if to prevent Lopahin's advances.

Event 1.28 (Leading Characters Lopahin and Ranevskaya)

LOPAHIN: Charlotta Ivanovna, show us some tricks!
RANEVSKAYA: Charlotta, show us some tricks!
CHARLOTTA: I don't want to. I wish to sleep. [*Goes out*]

Charlotta's entrance has enlivened the atmosphere. Conflict: Lopahin and Ranevskaya see Charlotta as a person who is constantly drawn to people. But to Charlotta, Ranevskaya and those around her are of no interest at all. (Note that later, in Act II, she does not take part in Ranevskaya's daily gatherings, and in her monologue (E2.1) she remarks, "One wants to talk and has no one to talk to...."

Lopahin's and Ranevskaya's action is to have Charlotta stay and join the company. Charlotta's action is to keep aside. Changing into a white dress, she celebrates Ranevskaya's return by herself.

Hints: Lopahin blocks Charlotta's passage. But she dodges him and, as if weary of Lopahin, leaves the stage.

Event 1.29 (Leading Character Lopahin)

> LOPAHIN: In three weeks' time we shall meet again. *[Kisses Lyubov Andreyevna's hand]* Goodbye till then—I must go. *[To Gaev]* Goodbye. *[Kisses Pishchik]* Goodbye. *[Gives his hand to Varya, then to Firs and Yasha]* I don't want to go. *[To Lyubov Andreyevna]* If you think over my plan for the cottages and make up your mind, then let me know; I will lend you fifty thousand. Think of it seriously.
>
> VARYA: *[Angrily]* Well, do go, for goodness sake.
>
> LOPAHIN: I'm going, I'm going. *[Goes out]*

It is time for Lopahin to go, but he still hasn't had a response to his plan from Ranevskaya.

Conflict between Lopahin and the group comprising Ranevskaya and Varya: Lopahin considers himself to be of great need to Ranevskaya, her savior. But they see him as a stranger who keeps interfering in matters he doesn't understand. He has already been told that his plan is unacceptable.

Lopahin's action is once again to remind the others of his presence. He is reluctant to leave, hoping to steer the conversation back to his plan. Ranevskaya ignores his hints while Varya hastens to get him out.

Hints: Lopahin haltingly kisses Ranevskaya's hand and slowly bids everyone farewell. He reluctantly leaves, looking back.

Event 1.30 (Leading Character Gaev)

GAEV: Boor. I beg pardon, though.... Varya is going to marry him, he's Varya's precious fiance.
VARYA: Don't talk nonsense, uncle.

Gaev is sick and tired of the unceremonious and self-assured Lopahin with his mad plan of destroying their family estate. And that is the man Varya loves and intends to let into their house! Conflict: Gaev sees himself as the head of the family who must uphold its interests. But to Varya, Gaev is a person not to be taken seriously. Now he again talks nonsense. Gaev's action aims to sober Varya up, to open her eyes. Varya's action is to silence her uncle. She is tired of groundless rumors about her imminent wedding (see E1.9).

Hints: Gaev embraces Varya and venomously introduces her to everyone present. Varya frees herself while paying no attention to his words.

Event 1.31 (Leading Character Ranevskaya)

RANEVSKAYA: Well, Varya, I shall be delighted. He's a good man.
PISHCHIK: He is, one must admit, a most worthy man. And my Dashenka...says too that...she says...various things. [*Snores, but at once wakes up*]

Given the family's current straits, Lopahin is an ideal match for the simple, industrious Varya. Conflict: Ranevskaya thinks that Varya is very fortunate and that things are turning out very well for her. But Varya sees her situation as hopeless, holding no promise for the future. She knows that Lopahin surely has no intention of marrying her, and she has no hopes for personal happiness (see E1.10, E1.11).

Ranevskaya's action is to support and encourage Varya. Varya's action is to avoid talk on the subject. Now is an unsuitable time for explaining anything to Ranevskaya, so Varya simply avoids responding.

Hints: Ranevskaya happily reaches her hands out to Varya, congratulating her. Pishchik, who has swallowed a lot of sedative pills, and is barely staying awake, lifts himself in the chair and voices his congratulations.

Event 1.32 (Leading Character Pishchik)

PISHCHIK: But all the same, honored lady, could you oblige me...with a loan of 240 rubles...to pay the interest on my mortgage tomorrow?

VARYA: *[Dismayed]* No, no!

RANEVSKAYA: I really have no money.

PISHCHIK: It will turn up. *[Laughs]* I never lose hope. I thought everything was over, I was a ruined man, and lo and behold—the railroad passed through my land and...they paid me for it. And something else will turn up again, if not today, then tomorrow.... Dashenka will win two hundred thousand...she's got a lottery ticket.

RANEVSKAYA: Well, we've finished our coffee, we can go to bed.

FIRS: *[Brushes Gaev, reprovingly]* You have got on the wrong trousers again! What am I do with you?

Pishchik is in dire straits, on the verge of losing his estate. He has already asked Ranevskaya for money but has been refused. Apparently in the bustle of her arrival Ranevskaya has failed to understand his situation. Conflict between Pishchik and a group comprising Ranevskaya and Varya: Pishchik thinks of himself as a friend of the family who simply cannot be refused. But to them he is a person indifferent to the misfortunes of others. Pishchik has already been told that Ranevskaya has no money; he knows their situation, yet he continues to pester them foolishly and spoil their evening. Pishchik's action is to keep pressing Ranevskaya in the hope of wearing her down. Varya's and Ranevskaya's action is to get rid of Pishchik.

Hints: Pishchik desperately tries to stay awake.

Analysis of The Cherry Orchard

Event 1.33 (Leading Characters Varya and Gaev)

VARYA: *[Softly]* Anya's asleep. *[Softly opens the window]* Now the sun's risen, it's not a bit cold. Look mamma, what exquisite trees! My goodness! And the air! The starlings are singing!

GAEV: *[Opens another window]* The orchard is all white. You've not forgotten it, Lyuba? That long path that runs straight, straight as an arrow, how it shines on a moonlight night. You remember? You've not forgotten?

RANEVSKAYA: *[Looking out of the window into the garden]* Oh, my childhood, my innocence! It was in this nursery I used to sleep, from here I looked out into the orchard, happiness waked with me every morning, and in those days the orchard was just the same, nothing has changed. *[Laughs with delight]* All, all white! Oh, my orchard! After the dark gloomy autumn, and the cold winter; you are young again, and full of happiness, the heavenly angels have never left you.... If only I could cast off the stone that weighs on my heart, if I only could forget the past!

GAEV: And the orchard will be sold to pay our debts; it seems strange....

RANEVSKAYA: See, our mother walking...all in white, down the path! *[Laughs with delight]* It is she!

GAEV: Where?

VARYA: Oh, don't mamma!

RANEVSKAYA: There is no one. It was my imagination. On the right there, by the path to the arbor, there is a white tree bending like a woman.... *[Enter Trofimov wearing a shabby student's uniform and glasses]* What a ravishing orchard! White masses of blossom, blue sky....

Ranevskaya prepares to go without ever mentioning the situation of the estate. Conflict between Ranevskaya and a group comprising Varya and Gaev: To them Ranevskaya is remote from their world, with other concerns and interests. Ranevskaya, for her part, sees herself as regaining her family and home and beginning life anew. At last she has returned to where she will find support and where people will help heal her psychological wounds and regain peace of mind.

Gaev's and Varya's action is to make Ranevskaya face up to reality. Ranevskaya's action is to get everyone to join the celebration of the beginning of her new life.

Hints: Ranevskaya lifts the petals of a blooming cherry tree off the window sill and starts to reminisce. Gaev, tactfully, reminds his sister of the sad present, and then himself loses a sense of reality.

Event 1.34 (Leading Character Trofimov)

TROFIMOV: Lyubov Andreyevna! *[She looks round at him]* I will just pay my respects to you and then leave you at once. *[Kisses her hand warmly]* I was told to wait until morning, but I didn't have the patience to wait any longer. ... *[Lyubov Andreyevna looks at him perplexed]*

VARYA: *[Through her tears]* This is Petya Trofimov.

TROFIMOV: Petya Trofimov, who was your Grisha's tutor.... Can I have changed so much? *[Lyubov Andreyevna embraces him and weeps quietly]*

Trofimov had been told not to appear before Ranevskaya today. Conflict between Trofimov and Ranevskaya and Varya: Trofimov thinks that meeting him will be a pleasant surprise for Ranevskaya. But to her he is a stranger who has invaded their family celebration. She has long since forgotten who he is. Varya, for her part, sees him as a callous egotist with no concern for others. She knows that Trofimov's appearance will remind Ranevskaya of her son's tragic death and mar the joy of her return.

Trofimov's action is to gain Ranevskaya's attention. He feels that after so many years there is no basis for Varya's anxieties. Ranevskaya's action is to determine who Trofimov is. Varya's action is to shame and chastise Trofimov.

Hints: Trofimov stands still, waiting for Ranevskaya to run to him joyfully. Ranevskaya inquiringly glances at Varya and Gaev.

Event 1.35 (Leading Character Ranevskaya)

GAEV: *[In confusion]* There, there, Lyuba.

VARYA: *[Crying]* I told you, Petya, to wait till tomorrow.

RANEVSKAYA: My Grisha...my boy...Grisha...my son!

VARYA: We can't help it, mamma, it is God's will.

TROFIMOV: *[Softly through his tears]* There...there.

RANEVSKAYA: *[Weeping quietly]* My boy was lost, drowned.... What for? What for, my friend.

Ranevskaya recognizes her dead son's tutor and is flooded with memories. (Later, in her "confession" in E2.6, Ranevskaya recalls that time: "To my misery, I loved another man, I took up with him, and immediately—it was my first punishment—the blow fell upon me, here, in the river...my boy was drowned...." From this passage it is apparent that Ranevskaya is convinced that her son's accidental death was punishment for her sins.)

Conflict between Ranevskaya and a group comprising Varya, Gaev, and Trofimov: Ranevskaya sees herself as a sinner who has suffered a terrible punishment, but to them she is a victim, an inconsolable mother still unable to come to terms with the loss of her child.

Ranevskaya's action is to withdraw into her personal life and problems. This is indicated by her words, "My boy was lost, drowned.... What for? What for, my friend." The group's action is to distract Ranevskaya and steer her away from sad memories.

Hints: See author's stage directions.

Event 1.36 (Leading Character Ranevskaya)

RANEVSKAYA: *[More quietly]* Anya is asleep in there, and I'm talking loudly...making this noise.... But, Petya? Why have you gotten so ugly? Why do you look so old?

TROFIMOV: A peasant woman in the train called me a mangy-looking gentleman.

RANEVSKAYA: You were quite a boy then, a pretty little student, and now your hair's gotten thin—and glasses. Are you really still a student? *[Goes toward the door]*

TROFIMOV: I seem likely to be a perpetual student.

RANEVSKAYA: *[Kisses her brother, then Varya]* Well, go to bed.... You've gotten old too, Leonid.

Ranevskaya suddenly realizes she has touched upon something no one but she can understand and which should not be brought up now. Conflict between Ranevskaya and Trofimov: Ranevskaya sees herself as out of sorts and unable to take part in the conversation. Trofimov thinks that Ranevskaya shows interest in him and seeks his company, because she asks Trofimov about himself.

Ranevskaya's action is to conclude the evening. She interrupts herself in mid-sentence, shifts the conversation to Trofimov, and leaves. Trofimov's action is to distract and comfort Ranevskaya. He pays no attention to her rather unflattering remarks—he is above that.

Hints: After a short pause, Ranevskaya straightens herself and absentmindedly converses with Trofimov while looking at Varya and Gaev. Trofimov squeezes out a few jokes which get no reaction from anyone.

Event 1.37 (Leading Character Pishchik)

PISHCHIK: *[Follows her]* I suppose it's time we were asleep.... Ugh! my gout. I'm staying the night.... Lyubov Andreyevna, my dear soul, if you could tomorrow morning...240 rubles....

GAEV: That's always his story.

PISHCHIK: 240 rubles...to pay the interest on my mortgage.

RANEVSKAYA: My dear man, I have no money.

PISHCHIK: I'll pay it back, my dear...a trifling sum.

RANEVSKAYA: Oh, well, Leonid will give it you.... You give him the money, Leonid.

GAEV: Me give him! Let him wait till he gets it!

RANEVSKAYA: It can't be helped, give it him. He needs it. He'll pay it back.

Analysis *of* The Cherry Orchard

[Lyubov Andreyevna, Trofimov, Pishchik and Firs go out. Gaev, Varya, and Yasha remain]

Ranevskaya retires without Pishchik having the money. The conflict is the same as in E1.32: Pishchik sees himself as a friend of the family who simply cannot be refused. But to them he is a person indifferent to the misfortunes of others. The attitude toward Pishchik is the same as earlier, but now the group with Ranevskaya includes Gaev instead of Varya. The actions of both sides are also the same: Pishchik continues to press Ranevskaya to lend him the money, keeping her from leaving, while Ranevskaya and Gaev try to get rid of him. Seeing that she is unable to do so, Ranevskaya shunts him off to her brother. Gaev immediately turns down Pishchik's request.

Hints: Pishchik is not letting Ranevskaya's hand go, kissing it from time to time. Gaev tries to keep a distance.

Event 1.38 (Leading Character Gaev)

GAEV: Sister hasn't got out of the habit of flinging away her money. *[To Yasha]* Get away, my good fellow, you smell of chickens.

YASHA: *[With a grin]* And you, Leonid Andreyevich, are just the same as ever.

GAEV: What? *[To Varya]* What did he say?

VARYA: *[To Yasha]* Your mother has come from the village; she has been sitting in the servants' room since yesterday, waiting to see you.

YASHA: What a pain!

VARYA: For shame!

YASHA: Just what I need. She might just as well have come tomorrow. *[Goes out]*

Although Ranevskaya has left, her valet remains with the masters and, inadvertently, overhears the conversation about his mistress. Conflict: To Gaev and Varya, Yasha is an impudent servant who has forgotten his place and his duties. But

Yasha thinks that his place is now with the masters rather than the servants. He is Ranevskaya's confidant, a person accustomed to a different way of life (see Anya's story in E1.9).

The action of Gaev and Varya, who has come to his assistance, is to put Yasha in his place. Yasha's action is to stand up for himself and assert his right to be with the masters.

Hints: Gaev sits down in the armchair; Yasha moves closer to him. Gaev speaks to Yasha without looking at him. Varya presses her attack on Yasha until he leaves.

Event 1.39 (Leading Character Gaev)

VARYA: Mamma's just the same as ever, she hasn't changed a bit. If she had her own way, she'd give away everything.

GAEV: Yes.... [*A pause*] If a great many remedies are suggested for some disease, it means that the disease is incurable. I keep thinking and racking my brains; I have many schemes, a great many, and it really means none. If we could only have inherited money from somebody, or marry our Anya to a very rich man, or we might go to Yaroslavl and try our luck with our aunt, the Countess. She's very, very rich, you know.

VARYA: [*Weeps*] If God would help us.

GAEV: Don't blubber. Aunt's very rich, but she doesn't like us. First, sister married a lawyer, not a nobleman....[*Anya appears in the doorway*] She married not a nobleman, and she behaved herself, you might say, not very virtuously. She is good, kind, nice, and I love her very much, but, however one allows for extenuating circumstances, there's no denying that she's an immoral woman. One feels it in her slightest gesture.

Ranevskaya, whose arrival carried such great hopes, is ruined and absorbed with her personal problems. No one but Gaev can handle the affairs of the estate.

Conflict: Gaev sees himself as head of the family with the burden of salvaging the estate. But to Varya he is a helpless talker, incapable of action. Varya knows that the estate cannot be saved. Gaev's action is to win Varya's confidence. He explains to Varya that he is doing his best to find a way out of the difficult situation in which they have been put by Ranevskaya. Varya's action is to refuse to support her uncle or discuss anything with him. After learning that Ranevskaya has no money, Varya has lost the last shred of hope of saving the estate.

Hints: Gaev has no plans, so he improvises. Varya sits deep in thought, not listening to Gaev.

Event 1.40 (Leading Character Anya)

VARYA: *[In a whisper]* Anya's in the doorway.

GAEV: What? *[A pause]* It's odd. I've got something in my right eye.... I suddenly can't see. And on Thursday when I was in the district Court... *[Enter Anya]*

VARYA: Why aren't you asleep, Anya?

ANYA: I can't get to sleep.

GAEV: My little one. *[Kisses Anya's face and hands]* My child.... *[Through his tears]* You are not my niece, you are my angel, you are everything to me. Believe me, believe....

ANYA: I believe you, uncle. Everyone loves you and respects you...but, uncle dear, you must be silent...simply be silent. What were you saying just now about my mother, about your own sister? Why did you say that?

GAEV: Yes, yes.... *[Puts her hands over his face]* Really, that was awful! My God, save me! And today I made a speech to the bookcase...so stupid! And only when I had finished, I saw how stupid it was.

VARYA: It's true, uncle, you ought to keep quiet. Don't talk, that's all.

ANYA: And if you could keep from talking, it would make things easier for you, too.

GAEV: I won't speak. *[Kisses Anya's and Varya's hands]* I'll be silent.

Anya's uncle has just made another stupid remark about her mother and is now trying to talk her into thinking nothing has happened. Conflict between Anya and Gaev: Anya sees herself as sufficiently grown up to have a say in family affairs. But to Gaev she is still a child, incapable of understanding his relations with her mother. Gaev does not discuss Ranevskaya's personal life with Anya.

Anya's action is to shame her uncle. Gaev's action is to work himself out of the predicament he has talked himself into, and smooth over the situation. He does this by acknowledging that he has spoken foolishly. Varya acts within the same group as Gaev, helping him get out of an unpleasant situation.

Hints: See author's stage directions.

Event 1.41. (Leading Character Gaev)

GAEV: Only this is about business. On Thursday I was in the district court; well, there was a large group of us there and we began talking of one thing and another, and this and that, and do you know, I believe that it will be possible to raise a loan on a promissory note to pay the interest to the bank.

VARYA: If the Lord would help us!

GAEV: I'm going on Thursday; I'll talk of it again. *[To Varya]* Don't blubber. *[To Anya]* Your mamma will talk to Lopahin; of course, he won't refuse her.... And as soon as you're rested you shall go to Yaroslavl to the Countess, your great-aunt. So we shall all set to work in three directions at once, and the business is in the bag. We shall pay off the interest, I'm convinced of it.... *[Puts a caramel in his mouth]* I swear on my honor, I swear by anything you like, the estate won't be sold. *[Excitedly]* By my own happiness, I swear it! Here's my hand on it, call me a rotten, no-good man if I let it come to auction! Upon my soul I swear it!

ANYA: *[Her equanimity has returned, she is quite happy]* How good you are, uncle, and how clever! *[Embraces her uncle]* I'm at peace now! Quite at peace! I'm happy! *[Enter Firs]*

Gaev has placated Anya and returned to the conflict interrupted by her entrance. Gaev's conflict with Varya: Gaev sees
himself as head of the family, responsible for salvaging the estate. Varya sees him as an incapable babbler.

Gaev's action is to dispel his nieces' apprehensions. Varya's
action is the same as in El.39, which is to avoid discussing
Gaev's plan. She no longer has any hope. Anya has no conflict
with Gaev: she believes in her uncle and fully supports him.

Hints: Gaev, embracing his nieces around the shoulders,
speaks mainly to Anya. Varya avoids looking at her uncle.

Event 1.42 (Leading Character Firs)

FIRS: *[Reproachfully]* Leonid Andreyevich, have you no
fear of God? When are you going to bed?

GAEV: Right away, right away.... You can go, Firs.
I'll...yes, I will undress myself. Well, children, bye-bye....
We'll talk about details tomorrow, but now go to bed.
[Kisses Anya and Varya] I'm a man of the eighties.... They
run down that period, but still I can say I have had to suf-
fer not a little for my convictions in my life. It's not for
nothing that the peasant loves me. One must know the
peasant! One must know how...

ANYA: At it again, uncle!

VARYA: Uncle dear, you'd better be quiet.

FIRS: *[Angrily]* Leonid Andreyevich!

GAEV: I'm coming, I'm coming.... Go to bed. Bank off two
sides into the side pocket! *[Goes out, Firs toddling after him]*

It is already five in the morning and everyone is tired, but
Gaev continues to talk and seems unable to stop. Conflict
between Gaev and Firs, who is later joined by Anya and
Varya: They see Gaev as a person who has lost all sense of
moderation. But Gaev is the hero of the day, he is victorious.
He has found a way to save the estate and has completely
calmed his frightened nieces.

The action of Firs, Anya, and Varya is to bring Gaev back
to normalcy. Gaev's action is to prolong his triumph and re-

main. He is basking in well-deserved success and attention.

Hints: Gaev loosely brushes Firs aside and continues to stand embracing Anya and Varya. Firs stands still and looks reproachfully at Gaev.

Event 1.43 (Leading Character Anya)

ANYA: My mind's at rest now. I don't want to go to Yaroslavl, I don't like my great aunt, but still my mind's at rest. Thanks to uncle. *[Sits down]*

VARYA: We must go to bed. I'm going. Something unpleasant happened while you were away. In the old servants' quarters, as you know, there are only the old servants: Efimushka, Polya, Yevstigney, and Karp. They began letting vagabonds in to spend the night—I said nothing. But all at once I heard they had been spreading a rumor that I gave them nothing but pea soup to eat. Out of stinginess, you know.... And it was all Yevstigney's doing.... Very well, I said to myself.... If that's how it is, I thought, wait a bit. I sent for Yevstigney.... *[Yawns]* He comes.... "How's this, Yevstigney," I said, "you could be such a fool as to?..." *[Looking at Anya]* Anitchka!... *[A pause]* She's asleep. *[Puts her hands around Anya]* Come to bed...come along! *[Leads her]* My darling has fallen asleep! Come.... *[They go]*

[Far away beyond the orchard a shepherd plays on a pipe. Trofimov crosses the stage and, seeing Anya and Varya, stands still]

VARYA: Sh! She's sleeping, sleeping. Come, my darling.

ANYA: *[Softly, half asleep]* I'm so tired.... Still those bells.... Uncle...dear...mamma and uncle....

VARYA: Come, my darling, come along.... *[They go into Anya's room]*

TROFIMOV: *[Tenderly]* My sunshine! My spring!

Anya believes in her uncle's plans and has calmed down: finally all their problems will be happily resolved. Conflict: Anya sees herself as an adult member of the family, helping to resolve important affairs on an equal footing with the others. But to Varya she is a trusting and naive child, believing in her uncle's fairy tales. Anya's action is to draw Varya into discussing their uncle's plans. Varya's action is to steer Anya away from business talk by speaking about domestic events.

In this event there is also an incidental conflict between Varya (leading character) and Trofimov. Trofimov was told that he should not show up today; he has not only come without permission but continues to hang around the house and may keep Anya from getting her night's rest. Conflict: Varya perceives Trofimov to be subservient and someone who is kept around the house out of charity. Trofimov considers himself to be independent and his own master. Varya's action is to get Trofimov out. Trofimov's action is to ignore Varya.

Hints: Anya sits down on the sofa and pulls Varya after her. Varya waves off the entering Trofimov, but Trofimov does not approach. He stands mesmerized by Anya.

19. Act II

A month or so has passed since the events of Act I. Several days ago Lopahin returned from Harkov, and now he spends all his time with Ranevskaya, trying to persuade her to resolve the problem of the profitless estate by leasing the land for country cottages.

Event 2.1 (Charlotta's Monologue)

The open country. An old chapel, long abandoned and fallen out of perpendicular; near it a well, large stones which have apparently once been tombstones, and an old garden seat. The road to Gaev's estate is seen. On one side rise dark poplars, and there the cherry orchard begins. In the distance a row of telegraph poles, and far, far away on the horizon there is faintly outlined a big city, visible only in very fine clear weather. It is near sunset. Charlotta, Yasha, and Dunyasha are seated on the garden seat. Epihodov is standing

87

nearby playing a guitar. All sit plunged in thought. Charlotta wears an old forage cap; she has taken a gun from her shoulder and is adjusting the buckle on the strap.

CHARLOTTA: *[Deep in thought]* I don't have a real passport of my own, and I don't know how old I am, and I always feel that I'm a young thing. When I was a little girl, my father and mother used to travel about to fairs and give performances—very good ones. And I used to jump somersaults and all sorts of things. And when papa and mamma died, a German lady took me and had me educated. Very well. I grew up and became a governess. But where I came from,and who I am, I don't know.... Who my parents were, maybe they weren't married.... I don't know. *[Takes a cucumber out of her pocket and eats]* I know nothing at all. *[A pause]* I want to talk so much and have no one to talk to.... I have nobody.

This a monologue—Charlotta does not try to communicate with other characters or obtain anything from them. This is also indicated by the author's comments, "All sit plunged in thought" and Charlotta is "deep in thought."

As noted before, an active monologue must have juxtapositions and contrasts in it. Otherwise it is lifeless and degenerates into either a monotonous declamation or an emotional embellishment of words.

Charlotta's monologue offers an idea of what troubles her: constant loneliness and a lack of purpose in her life. She has never known the meaning of home and family: with the circus she was always on the road, later she has lived among strangers. Charlotta knows nothing of herself or her parents. But she doesn't allow herself to become despondent. She looks for things in life that might bring happiness and solace: she had an interesting childhood, and although her parents died early, she was able to acquire a respectable profession. Charlotta views all this with a sense of humor, considering herself to be a rather remarkable person whose circumstances are unlike those of others; she doesn't even know her age.

Charlotta's monologue continues, with interruptions, until her exit.

Hints: Yasha and Dunyasha are sitting at one end of the bench while Charlotta is sitting at the other, half-turned away from them. Epihodov is standing next to Dunyasha, running his fingers over the guitar strings.

Event 2.2 (Leading Character Epihodov)

EPIHODOV: *[Plays on the guitar and sings]* "What care I for the noisy world! What care I for friends or foes!" How pleasant it is to play on the mandolin!

DUNYASHA: That's a guitar, not a mandolin. *[Looks in a hand-mirror and powders herself]*

EPIHODOV: To a man mad with love, it's a mandolin. *[Sings]* "Were her heart but aglow with love's mutual flame." *[Yasha joins in]*

CHARLOTTA: How awfully these people sing...foo. Like jackals.

DUNYASHA: *[To Yasha]* What happiness, though, to visit foreign countries.

YASHA: Yes, of course. I rather agree with you there. *[Yawns, then lights a cigar]*

EPIHODOV: That's comprehensible. In foreign countries everything has long since reached full complexion.

YASHA: That's so, of course.

EPIHODOV: I'm a cultivated man, I read remarkable books of all sorts, but I can never make out the tendency I am myself precisely inclined for, whether to live or to shoot myself, speaking precisely, nevertheless I always carry a revolver. Here it is.... *[Shows revolver]*

CHARLOTTA: I've had enough, and now I'm going. *[Puts on the gun]* Epihodov, you're a very clever man, and a very terrible one too, all women must be wild about you. Br-r-r! *[Goes]* These clever people are all so stupid; there's not a creature for me to speak to.... Always alone, alone, nobody belonging to me...and who I am, and why I'm on earth, I don't know.... *[Walks away slowly]*

EPIHODOV: Speaking precisely, not touching upon other subjects, I'm bound to admit about myself that destiny behaves mercilessly to me, as a storm to a little boat. If, let us suppose, I am mistaken, then why did I wake up this morning, to quote an example, and look round, and there on my chest was a spider of fearful magnitude...like this. *[Shows with both hands]* And then I take up a jug of kvass, to quench my thirst, and in it there is something in the highest degree unseemly of the nature of a cockroach. *[A pause]* Have you read Henry Thomas Buckle? *[A pause]* I am desirous of troubling you, Dunyasha, with a couple of words.

DUNYASHA: Well, speak.

EPIHODOV: I should be desirous to speak with you alone. *[Sighs]*

DUNYASHA: *[Embarrassed]* Well—only bring me my cape first. It's by the cupboard. It's rather damp here.

EPIHODOV: Certainly... I will fetch it.... Now I know what I must do with my revolver.... *[Takes guitar and goes off playing on it]*

YASHA: Two and twenty misfortunes! Between ourselves, he's a fool. *[Yawns]*

DUNYASHA: God grant he doesn't shoot himself. *[A pause]*

Today Epihodov is in the same company with Dunyasha who lately pays him no attention. Conflict: Epihodov considers himself to be a distinctive personality, a man of culture and education. But to everyone else he is a stupid, importunate nuisance.

Epihodov's action is to arouse people's curiosity and draw their attention. The action of his opponents is to get rid of him. Yasha and Dunyasha evade his attempts to strike up a conversation, while Charlotta ridicules him and goes away.

Hints: Dunyasha and Yasha ignore Epihodov; they avoid looking at him or getting into any kind of conversation with him. Epihodov takes Charlotta's remark as a compliment. This enlivens him even more, and he invites Dunyasha to talk in private.

Event 2.3 (Leading Character Dunyasha)

DUNYASHA: I became so restless, I worry all the time. I was a little girl when I was taken into our lady's house, and now I have quite grown out of peasant ways, and my hands are white, as white as a lady's. I'm such a delicate, sensitive creature, I'm afraid of everything. I'm so frightened. And if you deceive me, Yasha, I don't know what will become of my nerves.

YASHA: *[Kisses her]* You're a peach! Of course a girl must never forget herself; what I dislike more than anything is a girl being bad in her behavior.

DUNYASHA: I'm passionately in love with you, Yasha; you are a man of culture—you can give your opinion about everything. *[A pause]*

YASHA: *[Yawns]* Yes.... My opinion is this: if a girl loves anyone, that means that she has no morals. *[A pause]* It's pleasant smoking a cigar in the open air. *[Listens]* Someone is coming this way.... It's the gentlefolk.... *[Dunyasha embraces him impulsively]* Go home, as though you had been to the river to bathe; go by the path, or else they'll meet you and suppose I have had a date with you here. I can't stand it.

DUNYASHA: *[Coughing softly]* The cigar has made my head ache.... *[Goes off]*

[Yasha remains sitting near the chapel. Enter Lyubov Andreyevna, Gaev and Lopahin]

This event was examined in Part I. Dunyasha and Yasha have fallen in love and entered into a relationship. Their affair is at its peak, but Yasha has not proposed. Conflict: Dunyasha sees herself as an honorable girl who deserves respect and consideration. But to Yasha she is a girl of easy virtue with whom there is no need to stand on ceremony. She can have no claims on him because he has never given her cause for expectations.

Dunyasha's action is to draw Yasha into a frank conversation and determine his intentions. Dunyasha emphasizes her helplessness and bewilderment and points out that Yasha is responsible for her ambiguous position. Yasha's action is to define their relations. Far from wishing to make a commitment, he doesn't even want to be seen with Dunyasha.

Event 2.4 (Leading Character Lopahin)

LOPAHIN: You must make your mind once for all—there's no time to lose. It's quite a simple question. Will you consent to letting the land for building or not? One word in answer: yes or no? Only one word!

RANEVSKAYA: Who is smoking such horrible cigars here.... *[Sits down]*

GAEV: Now the railway line has been brought near, it's made things very convenient. *[Sits down]* Here we have been over and lunched in town. Yellow to the corner! I should like to go home and have a game....

RANEVSKAYA: You will have plenty of time.

LOPAHIN: Only one word! *[Beseechingly]* Give me an answer!

GAEV: *[Yawning]* What?

The conflict is between Lopahin and a group comprising Ranevskaya and Gaev. In two months the estate will be auctioned off, yet neither Ranevskaya nor Gaev has responded to Lopahin's plan, behaving as though he were proposing something trivial, not worthy of their attention.

Conflict: Lopahin sees himself as the savior of Ranevskaya's family, without whom they will all be ruined. But to Ranevskaya and Gaev he is an outsider who has nothing in common with their world.

Lopahin's action is to force them to talk business. He knows that the only way Ranevskaya can escape bankruptcy is to accept his plan. Ranevskaya's and Gaev's action is to sidestep the issue. Lopahin has already been told that his plan is absolutely unacceptable (E1.21), yet he stubbornly keeps insisting on it. Moreover, it is useless to explain anything to him, because he is incapable of understanding why it is impossible for them to destroy their family estate. All that is left for them is to ignore Lopahin or change the subject.

Hints: Ranevskaya has a bag with a purse, perfume, and a handkerchief. Lopahin is walking next to Ranevskaya while Gaev purposefully stays behind.

Event 2.5 (Leading Character Ranevskaya)

RANEVSKAYA: *[Looks in her purse]* I had quite a lot of money here yesterday, and there's scarcely any left today. My poor Varya feeds us all on milk soup for the sake of economy; the old folks in the kitchen get nothing but dried peas, while I waste money in a senseless way. *[Drops purse, scattering gold pieces]* There, they have all fallen out.... *[Annoyed]*

YASHA: Allow me, I'll pick them up. *[Collects the coins]*

RANEVSKAYA: Pray do, Yasha. And what did I go off to the town to lunch for.... Your restaurant's a wretched place with its music and tablecloth smelling of soap.... Why drink so much, Leonid? And eat so much? And talk so much? Today you talked a great deal again in the restaurant, and all so inappropriately. About the era of the seventies, about the decadents. And to whom? Talking to waiters about decadents!

LOPAHIN: Yes.

GAEV: *[Waving his hand]* I'm incorrigible; that's evident.... *[Irritably to Yasha]* Why is it you keep fidgeting about in front of us...

YASHA: *[Laughs]* I can't help laughing when I hear your voice.

GAEV: *[To his sister]* Either I or he....

RANEVSKAYA: Get along! Go away, Yasha.

YASHA: *[Gives Lyubov Andreyevna her purse]* Right away. *[Hardly able to suppress his laughter]* This minute.... *[Goes off]*

The conflict is between Ranevskaya, on one hand, and Gaev and Lopahin, on the other. This morning another telegram arrived in which Ranevskaya's former lover again begs her to return (see E2.7). Ranevskaya is quite distraught: she fears she may succumb to the temptation and return to Paris to the man she still loves. But this is of no concern to her brother who is preoccupied only with himself. In addition, Lopahin keeps pestering them with his stupid plan.

Conflict: Ranevskaya sees herself in a critical situation, greatly in need of attention and support. But to Gaev she is a capricious woman with no grip on herself. In the presence of Lopahin and her valet, she uses Gaev to vent her bad mood. Lopahin, for his part, sees Ranevskaya as a woman with no foresight, incapable of understanding what is most important for her now, and preoccupied with stupid things. Instead of thinking about how to save the estate, she keeps digressing into meaningless talk.

Ranevskaya's action is to draw attention to herself. She needs people and distraction. Gaev's action is to stop and subdue his sister. Lopahin's action is to regain Ranevskaya's attention. With his "Yes" he suggests that Ranevskaya has sidetracked the conversation from the only topic of importance.

In this event there is also an incidental conflict between Gaev and Yasha (Leading Character Gaev). Ranevskaya has spoiled her valet, who keeps hanging around in her presence and is an unintended witness of all her tantrums.

Conflict: Gaev sees himself as the master of the house who is responsible for maintaining order. But to Yasha, Gaev is a nobody. His mistress is Ranevskaya, and his place is at her side. Gaev's action is to point out the valet's place in the house. Yasha's action is to stand his ground against Gaev. He takes orders only from Ranevskaya.

Hints: Lopahin does not sit down. He stands next to Ranevskaya, letting her know that their conversation is not finished.

Event 2.6 (Leading Character Lopahin)

LOPAHIN: Deriganov, the millionaire, means to buy your estate. They say he is coming to the sale himself.

RANEVSKAYA: Where did you hear that?

LOPAHIN: That's what they say in town.

GAEV: Our aunt in Yaroslavl has promised to send help; but when, and how much she will send, we don't know....

LOPAHIN: How much will she send? A hundred thousand? Two hundred?

RANEVSKAYA: Oh, well.... Ten or fifteen thousand, and we must be thankful to get that.

LOPAHIN: Forgive me, but such reckless people as you are—such queer, unbusinesslike people—I never met in my life. One tells you in plain Russian your estate is going to be sold, and you seem not to understand it.

RANEVSKAYA: What are we to do? Tell us what?

LOPAHIN: I do tell you every day. Every day I say the same thing. You absolutely must let the cherry orchard and the land on building leases; and do it at once, as quick as may be—the auction's close upon us! Do understand! Once make up your mind to build cottages, and you can raise as much money as you like, and then you are saved.

RANEVSKAYA: Summer cottages and summer residents—forgive me saying so—it's so vulgar.

GAEV: There I perfectly agree with you.

LOPAHIN: I shall sob, or scream, or faint. I can't stand it! You've worn me out! *[To Gaev]* You're a woman!

GAEV: What?

LOPAHIN: A woman! *[Wants to leave]*

Ranevskaya and Gaev have no wish to discuss Lopahin's plan with him, because they think they can make do without him. Relations between the parties (i.e., the conflict) is the same as in E2.4: Lopahin sees himself as an expert, without whose advice Ranevskaya and Gaev would be completely ruined. But to them he is a stranger, remote from their world. Now, however, the actions of the parties are different. Lopahin's action is to point out to them their incompetence and helplessness. He shows that with the appearance of a wealthy competitor they have no hope of preserving the estate. Ranevskaya's and Gaev's action is to spurn all attempts to intervene in their affairs. First

95

they explain to Lopahin that there is nothing left for them but to attempt to purchase the estate at the auction in the name of their aunt ("What are we to do? Tell us what?"), but then they respond to his insistence by openly declaring that his plan is unacceptable—it is "vulgar."

Hints: Lopahin corners Ranevskaya and Gaev, forcing them to admit that their only choice is to follow his instructions.

Event 2.7 (Leading Character Ranevskaya)

RANEVSKAYA: *[In dismay]* No, don't go! Do stay, my dear! Perhaps we shall think of something!

LOPAHIN: What is there to think of?

RANEVSKAYA: Don't go, I entreat you! With you here it's more cheerful, anyway.... *[A pause]* I keep expecting something, as though the house were going to fall about our ears.

GAEV: *[In profound dejection]* Double shot to the corner.... White into the side pocket....

RANEVSKAYA: We have been great sinners....

LOPAHIN: You have no sins to repent to....

GAEV: *[Puts a caramel in his mouth]* They say I've eaten up my property in caramels. *[Laughs]*

RANEVSKAYA: Oh, my sins.... I've always thrown my money away recklessly like a lunatic. I married a man who made nothing but debts. My husband died of champagne—he drank dreadfully. To my misery I loved another man, I took up with him, and immediately—it was my first punishment—the blow fell upon me, here, in the river...my boy was drowned and I went abroad—went away forever, never to return, not to see that river again.... I shut my eyes, and fled, distracted, and he after me...pitilessly, brutally. I bought a villa at Menton, for he fell ill there, and for three years I had no rest day or night. His illness wore me out, my soul was dried up. And last year, when my villa was sold to pay my debts, I went to Paris and there he robbed me of everything and abandoned me for another woman. I tried to poison myself.... So stupid,

96

so shameful.... And suddenly I felt a yearning for Russia, for my country, for my little girl.... *[Dries her tears]* Lord, Lord, be merciful, forgive me my sins! Do not punish me more! *[Takes a telegram out of her pocket]* I got this today from Paris. He implores forgiveness, entreats me to return.... *[Tears the telegram]* I fancy there is music somewhere. *[Listens]*

GAEV: That's our famous Jewish orchestra. You remember, four violins, a flute and a double bass.

RANEVSKAYA: That still in existence? We ought to send for them one evening, and give a ball.

At last Lopahin's stupid plan has been put to rest and Ranevskaya can get back to what is really urgent—her personal problems.

Conflict between Ranevskaya and Lopahin and Gaev: Ranevskaya sees herself as being at a critical juncture in her life and requiring attention and support. Lopahin, for his part, sees her as a woman whose head is filled with foolish thoughts and who doesn't understand what is important for her. He is deeply offended by Ranevskaya's treatment of him: he keeps devoting time and energy in a sincere effort to save her, but instead of trying to understand his wonderful plan she keeps launching into foolish talk about sins. As for Gaev, he thinks his sister has forgotten herself and lost all sense of propriety. She shamelessly airs her personal affairs for all to hear. Note that this conflict is a continuation of the main conflict in E2.5.

Ranevskaya's action is to focus attention on herself and her personal problems. She is unhappy and has come here to start a new life, but no one is even trying to help. She must be among people, it doesn't matter who, as long as she is not alone with her thoughts and doubts.

Gaev's action is to distract his sister. First he tries to reduce everything to a joke, then he does not respond until, to his great relief, Ranevskaya mentions hearing sounds of music. Lopahin's action is to stay out of the conversation. He hasn't yet recovered after the preceding stormy scene, and besides, he isn't sure how to behave and what to say.

Hints: Ranevskaya sits Lopahin down on the bench next to her. Gaev, at a distance, is sitting on the stone, regarding nature. An actress should remember that the telegram is the object of her attention. This awareness gives a start to her "confession," to her cry for help to be stopped from returning to her lover.

Event 2.8 (Leading Character Lopahin)

LOPAHIN: *[Listens]* I can't hear.... *[Hums softly]* "For money the Germans will turn a Russian into a Frenchman." *[Laughs]* I did see such a piece in the theater yesterday, it was so funny.

RANEVSKAYA: And most likely there is nothing funny in it. You shouldn't look at plays, you should look at yourselves a little oftener. How gray your lives are, how much nonsense you talk.

LOPAHIN: That's true. One may say honestly, we live a fool's life. *[A pause]* My father was a peasant, an idiot; he knew nothing and taught me nothing, only beat me when he was drunk, and always with his stick. In reality I am just such another blockhead and idiot. I've learned nothing properly. I write a wretched hand. I write so that I feel ashamed before folks, like a pig.

RANEVSKAYA: You ought to get married, my friend.

LOPAHIN: Yes...that's true.

RANEVSKAYA: You should marry our Varya, she's a good girl.

LOPAHIN: Yes.

RANEVSKAYA: She came to us from a humble family, she's busy all day long, and what's more important, she loves you. And you have liked her for a long time.

LOPAHIN: Well? I'm not against it.... She's a good girl. *[A pause]*

Lopahin is surprised: Ranevskaya asked him to remain and

98

bared her soul to him, sharing such intimate details of her life as one might only with close family, say, a brother.

Conflict: Lopahin thinks he has been accepted by Ranevskaya as a close friend. Actually, to her he is a primitive person, devoid of tact. Ranevskaya is shocked by Lopahin's behavior: she is so distraught that her tears haven't even dried, and there he is laughing and singing a vulgar song.

Lopahin's action is to introduce himself, a new Lopahin whom Ranevskaya has not had a chance to discover. He speaks of his illiteracy without a trace of embarrassment, counting on Ranevskaya's understanding and consideration. Ranevskaya's action is to show Lopahin his place. He must act and behave naturally, as befits his standing, and stop trying to represent himself and to do things inappropriately. It would be best for him to set up a home and family by marrying a simple person, like himself.

Hints: Relieved, Lopahin stands up, cocks an ear, half-dancingly starts to hum, and then strolls with an air of a man who knows his worth.

Event 2.9 (Leading Character Gaev)

GAEV: I've been offered a place in the bank. Six thousand a year. Did you know?

RANEVSKAYA: You would never do for that! Stay as you are....

[Enter Firs with overcoat]

Ranevskaya sets Gaev on a level with Lopahin, noting how gray their lives are. Conflict between Gaev and Ranevskaya: Gaev considers himself to be an active and esteemed person. But to Ranevskaya he is just a talker, incapable of anything. He can't even support his sister at this difficult point in her life.

Gaev's action is to defend himself and demonstrate his true worth. He is the head of an old family, well known, and occupies a prominent position in the province's social and public life. It is no accident that he has just been offered an excellent position at the bank. Ranevskaya's action is to gain the upper hand over Gaev. All he says and does is nonsense, undeserving of attention.

When the conversation turns to the affairs of the estate, Lopahin joins in and supports Ranevskaya. As a result, the conversation becomes unpleasant for Gaev, and he quickly distracts attention to his nieces and Trofimov, who have just entered.

This event is interrupted in the middle by E2.10, caused by the entrance of Firs.

Hints: Hiding his hurt, Gaev reminds Ranevskaya who he is. Ranevskaya immediately cuts him short.

Event 2.10 (Leading Character Firs)

FIRS: Put it on, sir, it's damp.

GAEV: *[Putting it on]* You bother me, old fellow.

FIRS: You can't go on like this. You went away in the morning without leaving word. *[Looks him over]*

RANEVSKAYA: How you've aged, Firs!

FIRS: What is your pleasure?

LOPAHIN: You've aged, she said.

FIRS: I've had a long life. They were arranging my wedding before your papa was born.... *[Laughs]* I was the head footman before the emancipation came. I didn't take the freedom, I stayed with the masters.... *[A pause]* I remember what rejoicings they made and didn't know themselves what they were rejoicing over.

LOPAHIN: Those were fine old times. There was flogging at least.

FIRS: *[Not hearing]* To be sure! The peasants had their masters, and the masters had their peasants; but now everything's confused.

Everything is topsy-turvy, with a total breakdown of order. Now Gaev is getting out of hand. The conflict here is between Firs and a group comprising Ranevskaya, Gaev, and Lopahin. Firs sees himself as the only person who knows what a good, correct life should be like. The others see him as a blathering old man who should not be taken seriously.

Firs's action is to guide and admonish. He knows exactly how things should be. Ranevskaya's and Gaev's action is to be tolerant, not to counter or argue with Firs. Lopahin's action is to make fun of Firs.

Hints: Firs comes in, rests his cane, and walks toward Gaev while unfurling an overcoat. Gaev unwillingly dresses.

Event 2.9 (continued)

GAEV: Be quiet, Firs. I must go to town tomorrow. I have been promised an introduction to a general, who might let us have a loan.

LOPAHIN: You won't bring that off. And you won't pay the interest, you may rest assured of that.

RANEVSKAYA: That's all his nonsense. There are no such generals.

[Enter Trofimov, Anya, and Varya]

GAEV: Here come our people.

ANYA: Here mamma on the seat.

RANEVSKAYA: *[Tenderly]* Come here, come along. My darlings! *[Embraces Anya and Varya]* If you only knew how I love you both. Sit beside me, there, like that. *[All sit down]*

Event 2.11 (Leading Character Lopahin)

LOPAHIN: Our perpetual student is always with the young ladies.

TROFIMOV: That's not your business.

LOPAHIN: He'll soon be fifty, and he's still a student.

TROFIMOV: Drop your idiotic jokes.

LOPAHIN: Why are you so cross, you queer fish?

TROFIMOV: Leave me alone.

LOPAHIN: *[Laughs]* Allow me to ask you what's your idea of me?

TROFIMOV: I'll tell you my idea of you, Yermolay Alexeyevich. You are a rich man, you'll soon be a millionaire. Well, just as in the economy of nature a predatory animal is of use, who devours everything that comes in his way, so you too have your use. *[All laugh]*

Lopahin is in an excellent mood: Ranevskaya favors him and keeps him at her side. She has confided in him, rebuked her brother in his presence, and suggested that he marry her adopted daughter. And here comes one more member of the company, the student Trofimov, who regales them every evening with his "learned" discourses. Conflict between Lopahin and Trofimov: Lopahin considers himself an old friend of the intellectual Trofimov. But to Trofimov he is a tactless person who is alien in spirit. Lopahin keeps pestering him with his crude jokes which embarrass Trofimov in front of the others.

Lopahin's action is to set the tone and amuse the company. If Trofimov feels offended for some reason, Lopahin is prepared to offer himself as the butt of jokes. Trofimov's action is to get rid of Lopahin.

Hints: In answer to Petya's venomous joke, Lopahin laughs with the others, showing that he is not bothered in the least.

Event 2.12 (Leading Character Trofimov)

VARYA: Better tell us something about the planets, Petya.

RANEVSKAYA: No, let us go on with conversation we had yesterday.

TROFIMOV: What was it about?

GAEV: About human pride.

TROFIMOV: We had a long conversation yesterday, but we came to no conclusions. In human pride, in your sense of it, there is something mystical. Perhaps you are right from your point of view; but if one looks at it simply, without subtlety, what sort of pride can there be, what sense is there in it, if man in his physiological formation is very imperfect, if in the immense majority of cases he is coarse, dull-witted, profoundly unhappy? One must give up glorification of self. One should work, and nothing else.

GAEV: One must die in any case.

TROFIMOV: Who knows? And what does it mean—dying? Perhaps man has a hundred senses, and only the five we know are lost at death, and nothing else.

RANEVSKAYA: How clever you are, Petya!

LOPAHIN: *[Ironically]* Fearfully clever!

TROFIMOV: Humanity progresses, perfecting its powers. Everything that is beyond its ken now will one day become familiar and comprehensible; only we must work, we must with all our powers aid the seeker after truth. Here among us in Russia the workers are few in numbers as yet. The vast majority of the intelligentsia I know, seek nothing, do nothing, are not fit as yet for work of any kind. They call themselves intelligentsia, but they treat their servants as inferiors, behave to the peasants as though they were animals, learn little, read nothing seriously, do practically nothing, only talk about science, and know very little about art. They are all serious people, they all have severe faces, they all talk of weighty matters and air their theories, and yet the vast majority of us—ninety-nine percent—live like savages, at the least thing fly to blow and abuse, eat piggishly, sleep in filth and stuffiness, bedbugs everywhere, stench and damp and moral impurity. And it's clear all our fine talk is only to divert our attention and other people's. Show where to find the day nurseries there's so much talk about, and the public libraries? They only exist in novels: in real life there are none of them. There is nothing but filth and vulgarity and Asiatic apathy. I fear and dislike very serious faces. I'm afraid of serious conversations. We should do better to be silent.

Lopahin has just presented Trofimov as incapable of anything more serious than walking about with the young ladies. Conflict between Trofimov and a group comprising Ranevskaya, Gaev, and Lopahin: Trofimov thinks of himself as a person who sees the truth. But his opponents see him as a ridiculous young man whose head is filled with nonsense.

Trofimov's action is to present himself in a true light. For that he rather brusquely steers the conversation to a topic of his choice and, ignoring ironic comments, makes an angry speech exposing universal indifference to social injustice and to people who, like him, would fight against it. After setting forth his views, Trofimov concludes his speech with a colorful call for silence. The action of his opponents is to reduce it all to a joke and amuse themselves at Trofimov's expense. They cannot take either him or his ideas seriously.

Hints: Trofimov's speech is aimed at Anya. Her enthusiastic look feeds his oratory. Others glance smilingly at one another and good-naturedly joke at Trofimov's expense.

Event 2.13 (Leading Character Lopahin)

LOPAHIN: You know, I get up at five o'clock in the morning, and I work from morning to night; I've money, my own and other people's, always passing through my hands, and I see what people are around me. One has only to start doing anything to see how few honest decent people there are. Sometimes when I lie awake at night, I think: "Oh! Lord, you have given us immense forests, boundless plains, the widest horizons, and living here we ourselves ought really to be giants...."

RANEVSKAYA: You need giants.... They are only good in fairy tales; in real life they frighten us.

[Epihodov passes in the background playing the guitar]

RANEVSKAYA: *[Dreamily]* There goes Epihodov.

ANYA: *[Dreamily]* There goes Epihodov.

GAEV: The sun has set, ladies and gentlemen.

TROFIMOV: Yes.

The ne'er-do-well Trofimov has just called Lopahin a predator, and now he is trying to tell him how to live and for what purpose.

Conflict between Lopahin and a group comprising Ranevskaya, Gaev, and Trofimov: Lopahin considers himself to be a creator, a renovator of society. But to his opponents he is a money-grubbing businessman. He has already offered an example of his ideas by suggesting that the estate be destroyed to build summer cottages.

Lopahin's action is to present himself in a true light. He is the only one present who has something to say and something to teach. Alone among those present, he knows real life and is engaged in real, not imaginary, work. His opponents' action is to stop his discourse. Ranevskaya interrupts him in midsentence, and then the conversation drifts randomly—to Epihodov, who happens to be passing by, and to the setting sun.

Hints: An actor should remember that Lopahin's speech is his answer to unfair attacks.

Event 2.14 (Leading Character Gaev)

GAEV: [*Not loudly, but, as it were, declaiming*] O nature, divine nature, thou art bright with eternal luster, beautiful and indifferent! Thou, whom we call mother, thou dost unite within thee life and death! Thou dost give life and dost destroy....

VARYA: [*In a tone of supplication*] Uncle!

ANYA: Uncle, you are at it again!

TROFIMOV: You'd better cannon off the cushion!

GAEV: I'll hold my tongue, I will.

Trofimov and Lopahin have set forth their views on how one should live and what must be done for the good of society. To Gaev it is apparent that neither understands a thing about life.

Gaev's eloquent speech brings him into conflict with his nieces and Trofimov: Gaev sees himself as the only person there who knows the real meaning of life. But to the others he is a compulsive babbler.

Gaev's action is to destroy and vanquish his opponents and refute their mistaken views. In his opinion, any attempt to intervene in the natural course of events is useless and doomed to failure. Everything in the world occurs in accordance with the eternal laws of Nature which man can neither comprehend nor change. All that is left is to remain aloof and contemplate. The action of Anya, Varya, and Trofimov is to interrupt and silence Gaev.

Hints: Although Gaev is speaking to "divine nature," his speech is addressed to Trofimov and Lopahin.

Event 2.15 (Leading Character Ranevskaya)

> *[All sit plunged in thoughts. Perfect stillness. The only thing audible is the muttering of Firs. Suddenly there is a sound in the distance, from the sky, as it were—the sound of a breaking harp string, mournfully dying away]*
> RANEVSKAY: What is that?
> LOPAHIN: I don't know. Somewhere far away a cable has snapped and a cage has fallen in the mines. But somewhere very far away.
> GAEV: It might be a bird of some sort—such as a heron.
> TROFIMOV: Or an owl....
> RANEVSKAY: *[Shudders]* I don't know why, but it's horrid. *[A pause]*
> FIRS: It was the same before the calamity—the owl hooted and the samovar hissed all the time.
> GAEV: Before what calamity?
> FIRS: Before the emancipation. *[A pause]*
> RANEVSKAYA: Come, my friends, let us be going; evening is falling.

Today, on such a hard day for Ranevskaya, no one has come to her aid (see E2.5, E2.7). All evening they have been talking nonsense, and now the conversation has ceased completely. Suddenly a mournful sound, so consonant with her mental state, returns Ranevskaya to her troubles and finally spoils her mood.

Conflict between Ranevskaya and a group comprising Lopahin, Gaev, and Trofimov: Ranevskaya sees herself as troubled, at the threshold of misfortune. But to the others she is a person always governed by her moods. She is disturbed for no apparent reason by a sound. Ranevskaya's action is to keep people around her and regain their attention. She fears being alone with her thoughts. The group's action is to sustain the conversation.

This event also includes an incidental conflict between Firs (leading character) and the group of Lopahin, Gaev, and Trofimov. No one but Firs is capable of comprehending the meaning of that strange sound. Conflict: Firs sees himself as a worldly-wise person without whose knowledge and experience people would not know what to do. But to the others he is a blathering old man whose remarks should not be taken seriously. Firs's action is to open their eyes and forewarn them. His opponents' action is to be tolerant and not argue with Firs.

Hints: Firs is addressing Ranevskaya. He perceives her as the only person who is able to understand him.

Event 2.16 (Leading Character Ranevskaya)

RANEVSKAYA: *[To Anya]* There are tears in your eyes. What is it, darling? *[Embraces her]*
ANYA: Nothing, mamma; it's nothing.
TROFIMOV: There is somebody coming.

For some reason there are tears in Anya's eyes. Conflict: To Ranevskaya, Anya is a carefree child who can have no cause for worry. But Anya feels that she is now responsible for her mother and her life. Anya understands her mother better than anyone else; she sees her agitated state. This is what brings the tears to her eyes. Ranevskaya's action is to comfort and draw her daughter to herself. Anya's action is to avoid explaining anything.

Hints: Ranevskaya hugs Anya and falls behind the others.

Event 2.17 (Leading Character Wayfarer)

[The Wayfarer appears in a shabby forage cap and an overcoat; he is slightly drunk]

WAYFARER: Allow me to inquire, can I get to the station this way?

GAEV: Yes, go along that road.

WAYFARER: I thank you most feelingly. *[Coughing]* The weather is superb. *[Declaims]* My brother, my suffering brother!... Come out to the Volga! Whose groan do you hear?... *[To Varya]* Mademoiselle, vouchsafe a hungry Russian thirty kopecks....

[Varya utters a shriek of alarm]

LOPAHIN: *[Angrily]* There's a right and a wrong way of doing everything!

RANEVSKAYA: *[Confusedly]* Here, take this.... *[Looks in her purse]* I've no silver.... No matter—here's a gold piece for you....

WAYFARER: I thank you most feelingly! *[Goes off]*

[Laughter]

The slightly drunk Wayfarer has a stroke of good luck: he stumbles onto a group of partying gentry who doubtlessly will not refuse him a handout. Conflict between the Wayfarer, Gaev, and a group comprising Lopahin and Varya: The Wayfarer sees himself to be a respectable person deserving compassion and concern. But to Gaev, Varya, and Lopahin he is a drunken beggar who needs money for another drink. They are used to dealing with ordinary folk and can't be fooled. They know at a glance that this is not an unfortunate hungry person but a drunken lout.

The Wayfarer's action is to arouse sympathy and compassion. He does this by declaiming a few words from two popular poems about the unfortunate and dispossessed. Gaev's action is to stay aside, not to become involved. Lopahin's and Varya's action is to expose the Wayfarer and chase him off.

In this event there is an incidental conflict between Ranevskaya (leading character) and Lopahin.

Lopahin has, for no good reason, pounced on an unfortunate person. His behavior disgraces them all. Conflict: Ranevskaya considers herself to be put in an awkward position. But

to Lopahin she is a naive person who is remote from the realities of life. Ranevskaya who herself borrows from Lopahin
(see E2.18), gives away her last money to a drunk.

Ranevskaya's action is to stop Lopahin and offset his boorish conduct. Her upbringing does not allow her to accept
such ugly behavior. Lopahin's action is to retreat. He has no
intention of arguing with Ranevskaya, who does not understand with whom she is dealing.

Hints: Gaev, walking ahead of the others, politely answers
to the Wayfarer, and after passing him calmly waits for the
others, disregarding the Wayfarer's theatrics. The Wayfarer,
losing his balance, sways toward Varya who yelps and hides
behind Lopahin's back. Lopahin, barrel-chested, presses his
advance onto the Wayfarer until Ranevskaya interferes.

Event 2.18 (Leading Character Varya)

VARYA: *[Frightened]* I'm going away... I'm going away....
Oh, mamma, the servants have nothing to eat, and you
gave him a gold piece!

RANEVSKAYA: There's no doing anything with me. I'm so
silly! When we get home, I'll give you all I possess. Yermolay Alexeyevich, you will lend me some more!...

LOPAHIN: At your service.

RANEVSKAYA: Come, friends, it's time to be going. And
Varya, we have made a match of it for you. I congratulate
you.

VARYA: *[Through her tears]* Mamma, that's not a joking
matter.

Varya is astounded. She economizes on every kopeck, she is
unfairly accused of being miserly, and here Ranevskaya gives
away her last money to a drunk. The Wayfarer's laughter is
the last straw; the ever-patient Varya rebels—she will not tolerate Ranevskaya's outrageous actions anymore.

Conflict: Varya sees Ranevskaya as a selfish person who
never thinks of people close to her and is guided solely by her

whims. But Ranevskaya considers herself deeply devoted to home and family. She is ready to give her last kopeck for Varya and does everything to make her happy.

Varya's action is to expose Ranevskaya. For the first time she tells Ranevskaya all she thinks of her. Ranevskaya's action is to placate and distract Varya. In an effort to soothe her, Ranevskaya imprudently mentions her relationship with Lopahin, which causes a new outburst of indignation and accusations of insensitivity. But Ranevskaya was not joking: she is sincerely concerned about Varya's fate and has, in fact, already spoken to Lopahin about her (E2.8).

Hints: Ranevskaya hugs Varya and walks with her. She speaks purposely loud about Varya's engagement.

Event 2.19 (Leading Character Lopahin)

> LOPAHIN: "Ophelia, get thee to a nunnery...."
> GAEV: My hands are trembling; it's a long while since I had a game of billiards.
> LOPAHIN: "Ophelia! Nymph, in thy orisons be all my sins remembered."
> RANEVSKAYA: Come, it will soon be suppertime.
> VARYA: That man frightened me. My heart's still throbbing.
> LOPAHIN: Let me remind you, ladies and gentlemen: on August the twenty-second, the cherry orchard will be sold. Think about it!... Think about it!...
> *[All go off, except Trofimov and Anya]*

Ranevskaya has publicly announced Lopahin's engagement, though he has promised nothing to anyone.

Conflict between Lopahin and a group comprising Gaev, Ranevskaya, and Varya: Lopahin considers himself to be free from any commitments, a person whose conscience is clear. But to his opponents he is a vulgar person whose behavior toward Varya is beastly. Not only has he built up her hopes, but now he directs tactless jokes at Varya, who is in love with him.

Lopahin's action is to avoid any discourse on the subject. Picking up on Varya's words ("Mama, that's not a joking matter"), he pretends he is developing Ranevskaya's joke. Then he steers the conversation to the subject of the estate. His opponents' action is to distance themselves from Lopahin. They "do not hear" him and steer the conversation to another topic.

Event 2.20 (Leading Character Anya)

ANYA: *[Laughing]* I'm grateful to the wayfarer! He frightened Varya and we are left alone.

TROFIMOV: Varya's afraid we shall fall in love with each other, and for days together she won't leave us. With her narrow brain she can't grasp that we are above love. To eliminate the petty and transitory which hinder us from being free and happy—that is the aim and meaning of our life. Forward! Do not lag behind, friends!

ANYA: *[Claps her hands]* How well you speak! *[A pause]* It is divine here today!

TROFIMOV: Yes, it's glorious weather.

ANYA: Somehow, Petya, you've made me so that I don't love the cherry orchard as I used to. I used to love it so dearly. I used to think that there was no spot on earth like our garden.

TROFIMOV: All Russia is our garden. The earth is great and beautiful—there are many beautiful places in it. *[A pause]* Think only, Anya, your grandfather, and great-grandfather, and all your ancestors were slave-owners—the owners of living souls—and from every cherry in the orchard, from every leaf, from every trunk there are human creatures looking at you. Cannot you hear their voices?... To own human soul—it has degenerated you all, those who lived before and those who live now, so that your mother, you, your uncle, don't realize that you're living in debt, at the expense of those people whom you wouldn't let in through the front door.... We are at least two hundred years behind, we have really gained nothing yet, we have no definite attitude to the past, we do nothing but theorize or complain of depression or drink vodka. It is clear that to begin to live in the present we must first expiate our past; we must break with it; and we can expiate it only by suffering, by extraordinary unceasing labor. Understand that, Anya.

ANYA: The house we live in has long ceased to be our own, and I shall leave it, I give you my word.

TROFIMOV: If you have the house keys, fling them into the well and go away. Be free as the wind.

ANYA: *[In delight]* How beautifully you said it!

TROFIMOV: Believe me, Anya, believe me! I am not thirty yet, I am young, I am still a student, but I have gone through so much already! As soon as winter comes I am hungry, sick, careworn, poor as a beggar, and what ups and downs of fortune have I not known! And my soul was always, every minute, day and night, full of inexplicable forebodings. I have a foreboding of happiness, Anya. I see glimpses of it already....

ANYA: *[Pensively]* The moon is rising.

[Epihodov is heard playing still the same mournful song on the guitar. The moon rises. Somewhere near the poplars Varya is looking for Anya and calling "Anya! where are you?"]

TROFIMOV: Yes, the moon is rising. *[A pause]* Here is happiness—here it comes! It is coming nearer and nearer; already I can hear its footsteps. And if we never see it—if we may never know it—what does it matter? Others will see it!

VARYA'S VOICE: Anya! Where are you?

TROFIMOV: That Varya again! *[Angrily]* It's outrageous!

ANYA: Well, let's go down to the river. It's lovely there.

TROFIMOV: Yes, let's go. *[They go]*

VARYA'S VOICE: Anya! Anya!

At last Anya is alone with Petya Trofimov, who dreams of confessing his love for her. Conflict: Anya sees Trofimov as an irresolute, lovesick man who is behaving like a schoolboy. Trofimov, for his part, considers himself her teacher and mentor; he is "above love." In this he sees his strength and influence. Although he is in love he cannot permit himself to stoop to the trivial position of an admirer.

Anya's action is to steer Trofimov away from his usual topics and coax him into a romantic mood. This is why she interrupts his lengthy speeches with words like "we are left alone," "it is divine here today," "the moon is rising," and so forth. Trofimov's action is to ignore Anya's hints and avoid romantic topics. He hides behind his lofty rhetoric.

Hints: Anya is sitting on the bench. Trofimov is circling her, not able to bring himself to sit next to her.

20. Act III

Two months or so have passed since the events of Act II. Today, August 22, the day of the auction, a ball is being held in the house, and Ranevskaya must be home to receive the guests. Gaev, accompanied by Lopahin, has been gone since morning at the auction.

The aunt from Yaroslavl has sent the money requested, but everyone knows it is insufficient to purchase the estate. Only Ranevskaya and Gaev still hope for a lucky break, a miracle; all the rest have long since accepted the idea of the imminent loss of the estate.

Event 3.1 (Leading Character Pishchik)

A drawing room divided by the arch from a larger drawing room. A chandelier burning. The Jewish orchestra, the same that was mentioned in Act II, is heard playing in the anteroom. It is evening. In the larger drawing room they are dancing the grand chain. The voice of Semyonov-Pishchik: "Promenade à une paire!" Then enter the drawing room in couples first Pishchik and Charlotta Ivanovna, then Trofimov and Lyubov Andreyevna, thirdly Anya with the Post-Office Clerk, fourthly Varya with the Station Master, and other

guests. Varya is quietly weeping and wiping away her tears
as she dances. In the last couple is Dunyasha. They move
across the drawing room. Pishchik shouts: "Grand-rond, bal-
ancez!" and "Les cavaliers à genoux et remerciez vos dames!"

Firs, in a tail coat, brings in soda water on a tray. Pish-
chik and Trofimov enter the drawing room.

PISHCHIK: I am a full-blooded man; I have already had
two strokes. Dancing is hard work for me, but as they say,
if you're in the pack, you must bark with the rest. I'm as
strong, I may say, as a horse. My parent, who would have
his joke—may the Kingdom of Heaven be his!—used to
say about our origin that the ancient stock of the Semyonov-Pishchik was derived from the very horse that
Caligula made a member of the senate. *[Sits down]* But
I've no money, that's where the trouble is. A hungry dog
believes in nothing but meat. *[Snores, but at once wakes*
up] That's like me.... I can think of nothing but money.

TROFIMOV: There really is something horsy about your
appearance.

PISHCHIK: Well...a horse is a fine beast...a horse can be
sold.

[There is the sound of billiards being played in an adjoin-
ing room. Varya appears in the arch leading to the larger
drawing room]

TROFIMOV: *[Teasing]* Madame Lopahin! Madame Lopahin!

VARYA: *[Angrily]* Mangy-looking gentleman!

TROFIMOV: Yes, I am a mangy-looking gentleman, and
I'm proud of it!

VARYA: *[Pondering bitterly]* Here we have hired musicians
and nothing to pay them! *[Goes out]*

TROFIMOV: *[To Pishchik]* If the energy you have wasted
during your lifetime in trying to find the money to pay
your interest had gone to something else, you might in the
end have turned the world upside down.

PISHCHIK: Nietzsche, the philosopher, a very great and
celebrated man...of enormous intellect...says in his works
that one can make forged bank notes.

TROFIMOV: Why, have you read Nietzsche?

PISHCHIK: What next...Dashenka told me.... And now I am in such a position, I might just as well forge bank notes. The day after tomorrow I must pay 310 rubles—130 I have procured. *[Feels in his pockets, in alarm]* The money's gone! I have lost my money! *[Through his tears]* Where's the money? *[Gleefully]* Why, here it is behind the lining.... It has made me hot all over.

Pishchik is once again in dire straits, on the verge of ruin. He will lose his estate unless he urgently pays the interest on his mortgage. Conflict: Pishchik sees himself as a person deserving of the compassion and sympathy of others. But to Trofimov, people like Pishchik can only be despised. Material considerations play no part in Trofimov's life, and he is proud of this.

Pishchik's action is to impose his concerns on others and involve them in his problems. Pishchik has no doubt that penniless Trofimov understands him. Trofimov's action is to expose and ridicule Pishchik.

In the middle of this event Trofimov is distracted from the main conflict with Pishchik and is involved in an incidental conflict with Varya (leading character Trofimov).

All summer Varya has been taunting Trofimov, assuming he is pursuing Anya. With her narrow mind she is incapable of understanding that Trofimov is "above love" (see E2.19 and E3.6). Small wonder that she has only one dream in life—to marry the money-grubber Lopahin. Conflict: Trofimov believes he is absolutely superior to that primitive philistine Varya. To Varya, on the other hand, Trofimov is an indigent failed student with an inflated ego. Trofimov has nothing to his credit but bombastic rhetoric.

Trofimov's action is to needle and ridicule Varya. He calls her "Madam Lopahin" to stress her philistine essence. Varya's action is to get rid of Trofimov. She is sick and tired of his stupid attacks.

Hints: Trofimov and Pishchik approach the table which has bottles of mineral water and appetizers. Pishchik greedily gulps down the water, wipes the sweat off his face, pops a few buttons open, and sits down on the chair. Trofimov walks around the table picking appetizers. Varya enters, checks over the table, and carries out empty plates.

Event 3.2 (Leading Character Ranevskaya)

> *[Enter Ranevskaya and Charlotta Ivanovna]*
> RANEVSKAYA: *[Hums the Lezghinka]* Why is Leonid so long? What can he be doing in town? *[To Dunyasha]* Offer the musicians some tea.
> TROFIMOV: The sale hasn't taken place, most likely.
> RANEVSKAYA: It's the wrong time to have the orchestra, and the wrong time to give a ball. Well, never mind. *[Sits down and hums softly]*

It is already past nine o'clock, the sale is long over, but Gaev hasn't yet returned. Ranevskaya sees this as a bad omen.

Conflict between Ranevskaya and Trofimov: Ranevskaya thinks she needs special attention today. But to Trofimov she is a person inhabiting a world of illusions and refusing to acknowledge the real state of affairs. Ranevskaya is waiting in flustered anticipation, though actually nothing unexpected is happening. The estate has long since been lost, and today's auction is no more than a formality (see E3.6, where Trofimov tells her this directly).

Ranevskaya's action is to draw people to her side. She is troubled and can't help voicing her grief. Trofimov's action is to avoid discussing the auction. He shrugs it off with a meaningless phrase.

Hints: Ranevskaya is humming a Caucasian dance Lezghinka; its fast, jumping rhythm reflects her emotional state. In her hands is a fan which she is constantly folding and unfolding. Trofimov, in passing and continuing to chew something, answers Ranevskaya.

Event 3.3 (Leading Character Charlotta)

CHARLOTTA: *[Gives Pishchik a pack of cards]* Here's a pack of cards. Think of any card you like.

PISHCHIK: I've thought of one.

CHARLOTTA: Shuffle the pack now. That's right. Give it here, my dear Mr. Pishchik. Ein, zwei, drei—now look, it's in your breast pocket.

PISHCHIK: *[Taking a card out of his breast pocket]* The eight of spades! Perfectly right! *[Wonderingly]* Fancy that now!

CHARLOTTA: *[Holding the pack of cards in her hands, to Trofimov]* Tell me quickly which is the top card.

TROFIMOV: Well, the queen of spades.

CHARLOTTA: It is! *[To Pishchik]* Well, which card is uppermost?

PISHCHIK: The ace of hearts.

CHARLOTTA: It is! *[Claps her hands, pack of cards disappears]* Ah! what lovely weather it is today!

[A mysterious feminine voice which seems coming out of the floor answers her. "Oh, yes, it's magnificent weather, madam"]

CHARLOTTA: You are my perfect ideal.

VOICE: And I greatly admire you too, madam.

STATION MASTER: *[Applauding]* The lady ventriloquist— bravo!

PISHCHIK: *[Wonderingly]* Fancy that now! Most enchanting Charlotta Ivanovna. I'm simply in love with you.

CHARLOTTA: In love? *[Shrugging shoulders]* What do you know of love? Guter Mensch, aber schlechter Musikant.

TROFIMOV: *[Pats Pishchik on the shoulder]* Such a horse....

CHARLOTTA: Attention, please! Another trick! *[Takes a rug from a chair]* Here's a very good rug; I want to sell it. *[Shaking it out]* Doesn't anyone want to buy it?

PISHCHIK: *[Wonderingly]* Fancy that!

CHARLOTTA: Ein, zwei, drei! *[Quickly picks up rug she has dropped; behind the rug stands Anya; she makes a curtsey, runs to her mother, embraces her and runs back into the larger drawing room amidst general enthusiasm]*

RANEVSKAYA: *[Applauds]* Bravo! Bravo!

CHARLOTTA: Now again! Ein, zwei, drei! *[Lifts up the rug; behind the rug stands Varya, bowing]*

PISHCHIK: *[Wonderingly]* Fancy that now!

CHARLOTTA: That's the end. *[Throws the rug at Pishchik, makes a curtsey, runs into the larger drawing room]*

PISHCHIK: *[Hurries after her]* Mischievous creature! Fancy! *[Goes out]*

The ball is in progress, but the mood is far from festive. The mistress of the house can think only of the auction while Pishchik talks all evening only about money (E3.1). Conflict between Charlotta and Pishchik: Charlotta sees him as a person with no interests or spiritual needs (note that Trofimov joins Charlotta in this, calling Pishchik "a horse"). But Pishchik considers himself a spirited person, the soul of any company. Today, too, he has been making merry all evening and leading the dances.

Charlotta's action is to entice, stir, and excite Pishchik. Pishchik's action is to respond to her flirtation and show himself off to best advantage.

Hints: Ranevskaya is sitting by herself, not taking part in these amusements. She lights up only when Anya comes over. See also author's stage directions.

Event 3.4 (Leading Character Ranevskaya)

RANEVSKAYA: And still Leonid doesn't come. I can't understand what he's doing in the town so long! Why, everything must be over by now. The estate is sold, or the sale has not taken place. Why keep us so long in suspense?

VARYA: *[Trying to console her]* Uncle's bought it. I feel sure of that.

TROFIMOV: *[Ironically]* Oh, yes.

VARYA: Great-aunt sent him an authorization to buy it in her name, and transfer the debt. She's doing it for Anya's sake. And I'm sure God will help us and uncle will buy it.

RANEVSKAYA: My aunt in Yaroslavl sent fifteen thousand

to buy the estate in her name, she doesn't trust us—but that's not enough even to pay the interest. *[Hides her face in her hands]* My fate is being sealed today, my fate....

TROFIMOV: *[Teasing Varya]* Madame Lopahin!

VARYA: *[Angrily]* Perpetual student! Twice already you've been expelled from the University.

All reasonable deadlines have passed, but Gaev still hasn't returned. The conflict between Ranevskaya and Varya is no different from Ranevskaya's conflict with Trofimov in E3.2: she sees herself as someone needing special attention, but to Varya she is someone who thinks only of herself. Today they are having an absurd ball, and its responsibilities fall entirely upon Varya's shoulders. Ranevskaya's action is to keep Varya at her side. Varya's action is to get free and leave. Therefore she somehow tries to calm Ranevskaya.

Trofimov is amused: Varya believes in the impossible, that Gaev will purchase the estate. This leads to an incidental conflict: Trofimov sees his obvious superiority over the mediocre Varya, while she sees him as a fool incapable of understanding how to behave in the circumstances. Trofimov's action is to ridicule Varya. Varya's action is to put down Trofimov. She once again voices her firm conviction that Gaev will purchase the estate; then, seeing that Trofimov persists, points out that it is not for nothing that fools like him become university dropouts.

Hints: Ranevskaya repeatedly gets up and sits down. Varya picks up and folds the blanket, then rearranges the chairs which were moved during Charlotta's performance. Trofimov is waiting for the dances to begin.

Event 3.5 (Leading Character Ranevskaya)

RANEVSKAYA: Why are you angry, Varya? He's teasing you about Lopahin. Well, what of that? Marry Lopahin if you like, he's a good, interesting man. If you don't want to, don't. Nobody compels you, darling....

VARYA: I must tell you plainly, mamma, I look at the matter seriously. He's a good man, I like him.

RANEVSKAYA: Well, marry him. I can't see what you're waiting for!

VARYA: Mamma. I can't propose to him myself. For the last two years, everyone's been talking to me about him. Everyone talks; but he says nothing or else makes a joke. I see what it means. He's growing rich, he's absorbed in business, he has no thoughts for me. If I had money, were it ever so little, if I had only a hundred rubles, I'd throw everything up and go far away. I would go into a nunnery.

TROFIMOV: Heavenly!

VARYA: *[To Trofimov]* A student ought to be intelligent! *[In a soft tone with tears]* How ugly you've gotten, Petya! How old you look! *[To Ranevskaya, no longer crying]* But I can't do without work, mamma; I must have something to do every minute.

[Enter Yasha]

YASHA: *[Hardly restraining his laughter]* Epihodov has broken a billiard cue!... *[Goes out]*

VARYA: What is Epihodov doing here? Who allowed him to play billiards? I can't understand these people.... *[Goes out]*

For some reason Trofimov's harmless joke has angered Varya. She does not even realize how fortunate she is to be able to marry Lopahin. Conflict: Ranevskaya sees Varya as hidebound and irresolute, someone who does not understand how to manage her life. But Varya sees herself at a dead end, with no prospects for the future. She has long since lost hope of marrying Lopahin (see E1.10) and will soon be deprived of her last solace, work around the house.

Ranevskaya's action is to guide and encourage Varya, who simply doesn't understand where her happiness lies. Now, when they are losing their estate, marriage to Lopahin would be a great way out for the dowerless Varya. Varya's action is to bring Ranevskaya to her senses.

Trofimov's ironic comments distract Varya from Ranevskaya. She interrupts her action and enters an incidental conflict. This conflict does not differ from that in E3.4. For Trofimov (leading character of the incidental conflict), Varya's remark about leaving for the monastery is just another testimony of her primitiveness. Conflict: Trofimov thinks he can see through Varya, but to her he is a plain fool with no understanding of anything.

Trofimov's action is to taunt Varya. Varya's action is to humiliate and denounce Trofimov. With tears in her eyes she pityingly tells him how foolish, old, and unattractive he is, clearly suggesting that it is useless for him to pursue Anya. After finishing with Trofimov, Varya returns to the interrupted conflict with Ranevskaya.

Hints: Ranevskaya's remark about marriage stops Varya as she is just about to leave.

Event 3.6 (Leading Character Ranevskaya)

RANEVSKAYA: Don't tease her, Petya. You see she has grief enough without that.

TROFIMOV: She is so zealous, meddling in what's not her business. All the summer she's given Anya and me no peace. She's afraid of a love affair between us. What's it to do with her? Besides, I have given no grounds for it. Such triviality is not in my line. We are above love!

RANEVSKAYA: And I suppose I am beneath love. *[Very uneasily]* Why is it Leonid's not here? If only I could know whether the estate is sold or not! It seems such an incredible calamity that I really don't know what to think. I am distracted... I shall scream in a minute... I shall do something stupid. Save me, Petya, say something, say...

TROFIMOV: What does it matter whether the estate is sold today or not? That's all done with long ago. There's no turning back, the path is overgrown. Don't worry yourself, dear Lyubov Andreyevna. You mustn't deceive yourself; for once in your life you must face the truth!

RANEVSKAYA: What truth? You see where the truth lies, but I seem to have lost my sight, I see nothing. You settle every great problem so boldly, but tell me, my dear boy, isn't it because you're young—because you haven't yet understood one of your problems through suffering? You look forward boldly, and isn't it that you don't see and don't expect anything dreadful because life is still hidden from your young eyes? You're bolder, more honest, deeper than we are, but think, be just a little magnanimous, have pity on me. I was born here, my father and mother lived here, my grandfather lived here, I love this house. I can't conceive of my life without the cherry orchard, and if it really must be sold, then sell me with the orchard.... *[Embraces Trofimov, kisses him on the forehead]* My son was drowned here.... *[Weeps]* Pity me, my dear kind man.

TROFIMOV: You know I feel for you with all my heart.

RANEVSKAYA: But that should have been said differently, so differently.... *[Takes out her handkerchief, telegram falls on the floor]* My heart is so heavy today. It's so noisy here, my soul is quivering at every sound, I'm shuddering all over, but I can't go away. I'm afraid of silence, I'm afraid to be alone. Don't be hard on me, Petya.... I love you as though you were one of ourselves. I would gladly let you marry Anya—I swear I would—only, my dear, you must take your degree. You do nothing, you're simply tossed by fate from place to place. It is so strange, isn't it? And you must do something with your beard to make it grow somehow.... *[Laughs]* You look so funny!

TROFIMOV: *[Picks up the telegram]* I've no wish to be a beauty.

RANEVSKAYA: That's a telegram from Paris. I get one every day. One yesterday and one today. That savage creature is ill again, he's in trouble again. He begs forgiveness, beseeches me to go, and really I ought to go to Paris to see him. You look shocked, Petya. What am I to do, my dear, what I am to do? He is ill, he is alone and unhappy, and who'll look after him, who'll keep him from doing the wrong things, who'll give him his medicine at the right time? And why hide it or be silent? I love him, that's clear. I love him, I love him.... He's a millstone about my neck, I'm going to the bottom with him, but I love that stone and can't live without it.

[Presses Trofimov's hand] Don't think ill of me, Petya, don't tell me anything, don't tell me....

Trofimov understands neither what is happening in the house nor Ranevskaya's emotional state. This is a repetition of the conflict in E3.2: Ranevskaya sees herself as a person who today needs special attention. But to Trofimov she is a person living in an illusory world and refusing to reckon with the real state of affairs.

Ranevskaya's action is to find common language with Trofimov and win him over. She must be distracted in order to fill the time until Gaev's return. For that reason it doesn't matter whether Ranevskaya talks to him about Varya, herself, or him. Trofimov's action is to shake her off and not be drawn into the discussion. His views do not coincide with Ranevskaya's; furthermore, he has no desire to reeducate and dissuade her. The ball is going on, and Trofimov would prefer to be with Anya.

Hints: Ranevskaya aims to seat Trofimov next to her while he, shifting from foot to foot, waits for an opportune moment to leave.

Event 3.7 (Leading Character Trofimov)

TROFIMOV: *[Through his tears]* For God's sake, forgive my frankness: why, he robbed you!

RANEVSKAYA: No! No! No! You mustn't speak like that.... *[Covers her ears]*

TROFIMOV: He is a wretch! You're the only person that doesn't know it! He's a petty scoundrel, a nonentity!

RANEVSKAYA: *[Getting angry, but speaking with restraint]* You're twenty-six or twenty-seven years old, but you're still a schoolboy!

TROFIMOV: Just as you like!

RANEVSKAYA: You should be a man at your age! You should understand what love means! And you ought to be in love yourself! You ought to fall in love! *[Angrily]* Yes, yes, and it's not purity in you, you're simply a prude, a ridiculous crank, a freak.

TROFIMOV: *[In horror]* The things she's saying!

RANEVSKAYA: "I am above love!" You're not above love, but simply as our Firs here says, you are a "good-for-nothing." At your age not to have a mistress!

TROFIMOV: *[In horror]* This is awful! The things she is saying! *[Goes rapidly into the larger drawing room, clutching his head]* This is awful.... I can't stand it, I'm going.... *[Goes off, but at once returns]* All is over between us! *[Goes off into the anteroom]*

Ranevskaya has just demonstrated a total lack of understanding of life and people: she intends to do another awful thing—return to her lover.

Conflict: Trofimov thinks of himself as a man of honor, a friend of the family who should not keep quiet in such a situation. But Ranevskaya sees him as a person who has overstepped his boundaries, an egoist. Today, during this terrible moment in the life of their family, when she needs sympathy and support more than ever, Trofimov pours more salt in her wounds.

Trofimov's action is not to retreat but to move straight ahead at any cost. As a result, he fails in his action and flees in panic. Ranevskaya's action is to shut him up using any means available.

Hints: Trofimov is standing, completely at a loss, then quickly leaves, his walk bordering on a run.

Event 3.8 (Leading Character Ranevskaya)

RANEVSKAYA: *[Shouts after him]* Petya! Wait a minute! You funny creature! I was joking! Petya! *[There is a sound of somebody running quickly downstairs and suddenly falling with a crash. Anya and Varya scream, but there is a sound of laughter at once]* What has happened?

[Anya runs in]

ANYA: *[Laughing]* Petya's fallen downstairs! *[Runs out]*

RANEVSKAYA: What a queer fellow that Petya is....

[The Station Master stands in the middle of the larger room and reads The Sinful Woman *by Alexey Tolstoy.*

They listen to him, but before he has recited many lines, strains of a waltz are heard from the anteroom and the reading is broken off. All dance. Trofimov, Anya, Varya, and Ranevskaya come in from the anteroom]
RANEVSKAYA: Come, Petya—come pure heart! I beg your pardon. Let's have a dance! *[Dances with Petya]*

Trofimov apparently got what he deserved for his ill-advised behavior. Conflict: Ranevskaya sees him as someone who is unjustly upset with her. But Trofimov is above petty resentment: he knows his worth and cannot be hurt by Ranevskaya's senseless attacks at a time when she has no idea what she is saying or doing.

Ranevskaya's action is to placate Trofimov and reestablish their relationship. Trofimov's action is to avoid any settling of scores. Despite what has happened, he goes to dance with Ranevskaya.

Hints: Ranevskaya hurries after Trofimov and returns arm in arm with him. Trofimov does not look or talk with Ranevskaya while dancing with her. (Regarding the poem *The Sinful Woman,* see Appendix II.)

Event 3.9 (Leading Character Firs)

[Anya and Varya dance. Firs comes in, puts his stick down near the side door. Yasha also comes into the drawing room and looks on at the dancing]
YASHA: What is it, old man?
FIRS: I don't feel well. In old days we used to have generals, barons, and admirals dancing at our balls, and now we send for the post-office clerk and the station master and even they're not overanxious to come. I am getting feeble. The old master, the grandfather, used to give sealing wax for all complaints. I have been taking sealing wax for twenty years or more. Perhaps that's what keeps me alive.
YASHA: You bore me, old man! *[Yawns]* It's time you were done with.
FIRS: Ach, you're a good-for-nothing! *[Mutters]*

125

Firs is in a melancholy mood: today's gathering is quite unlike a real ball. But Yasha, standing nearby, is incapable of understanding that. Conflict: Firs thinks he has something to say and something to teach. But to Yasha he is a senile old man, babbling nonsense. Firs's action is to share experience and enlighten. Yasha's action is to get rid of Firs.

Hints: Yasha is so excited by the ball that he is speaking even to Firs, whom he despises. Firs is trying to stand straight and disguise his poor health.

Event 3.10 (Leading Character Ranevskaya)

[Trofimov and Ranevskaya dance in the larger room and then onto the stage]

RANEVSKAYA: Merci. I'll sit down a little. *[Sits down]* I'm tired.

[Enter Anya]

ANYA: *[Excitedly]* There's a man in the kitchen who has been saying that the cherry orchard's been sold today.

RANEVSKAYA: Sold to whom?

ANYA: He didn't say to whom. He's gone away.

[She dances with Trofimov, and they go off into the larger room]

Anya, all excited, brings the terrible news: the estate has been sold. Ranevskaya sees Anya as a person who, like herself, is deeply concerned with all that is happening. But Anya has long since accepted the fact that the estate is lost, and she is prepared to start a new life (see E2.20).

Ranevskaya's action is to keep Anya at her side. Anya's action is to avoid discussion. The ball continues, and she wants to dance.

Hints: Anya grabs Trofimov's hand and drags him onto the dance floor. She avoids Ranevskaya for she feels unable to console her.

Event 3.11 (Leading Character Yasha)

YASHA: There was an old man gossiping there, a stranger.

FIRS: Leonid Andreyevich isn't here yet, he hasn't come back. He has a light overcoat on, he'll catch a cold. Ach! These foolish young people.

RANEVSKAYA: I feel as though I should die. Go, Yasha, find out to whom it has been sold.

YASHA: But he went away long ago, that old man. [*Laughs*]

RANEVSKAYA: [*With slight vexation*] What are you laughing at? What are you so happy about?

YASHA: Epihodov is so funny. He's a silly fellow, two and twenty misfortunes.

They are having a wonderful ball, but stupid Anya has worried Ranevskaya for no reason. Conflict: Yasha considers himself to be the guardian of his mistress's interests, but to Ranevskaya he is a fool; he doesn't understand what is happening. Yasha's action is to distract Ranevskaya. Ranevskaya's action is to put some sense into Yasha, to wake him up to reality.

Hints: Yasha, speaking to Ranevskaya, does not stop looking at the dancers. He laughs at the sight of strutting Epihodov.

Event 3.12 (Leading Character Ranevskaya)

RANEVSKAYA: Firs, if the estate is sold, where will you go?

FIRS: Where you bid me, there I'll go.

RANEVSKAYA: Why do you look like that? Are you ill? You ought to be in bed....

FIRS: [*Ironically*] Me go to bed, and who's to wait here? Who's to see to things without me? I'm the only one in all the house.

Like Yasha, Firs also fails to understand what is happening. He keeps mumbling some nonsense about a coat. Conflict: Ranevskaya sees Firs as a senile old man, of no use to anyone. But Firs continues to regard himself as indispensable in the house. He is ready to follow Ranevskaya's family anywhere.

Ranevskaya's action is to prod Firs and awaken him to a realization of what is happening. Firs's action is to keep everything in order.

Hints: Firs is picking up and placing dirty dishes and empty bottles on a tray.

Event 3.13 (Leading Character Yasha)

YASHA: *[To Ranevskaya]* Lyubov Andreyevna, permit me to make a request of you; if you go back to Paris again, be so kind as to take me with you. It's positively impossible for me to stay here. *[Looking about him; in an undertone]* There's no need to say it, you see for yourself—an uncivilized country, the people have no morals, and then the dullness! The food in the kitchen's abominable, and then Firs runs after one muttering all sort of unsuitable words. Take me with you, please do!

Senile Firs is again talking nonsense, claiming he alone is capable of seeing to things in the house. Conflict: Yasha sees himself as a martyr unable to stand the awful situation any longer. But to Ranevskaya he is a fool who doesn't understand what is happening around him (see E3.11). Yasha's action is to gain Ranevskaya's support. Ranevskaya's action is to ignore him completely.

Hints: Yasha is distracted from the ball and walks over to sitting Ranevskaya.

Event 3.14 (Leading Character Pishchik)

[Enter Pishchik]
PISHCHIK: Allow me to ask you...for a waltz, my dear lady.... *[Ranevskaya goes with him]* Enchanting lady, I really must borrow of you just 180 rubles.... *[Dances]* Only 180 rubles.... *[They pass into the larger room]*
YASHA: *[Hums softly]* "Can you comprehend the stirring of my soul...."
[In the larger drawing room, a figure in a gray top hat and checked trousers is gesticulating and jumping about. Shouts of "Bravo, Charlotta Ivanovna!"]

All evening Pishchik has been unsuccessfully pestering Ranevskaya to lend him money. Now, when she is alone, is a convenient moment to renew his request.

Conflict: Pishchik considers himself an old friend of the family experiencing temporary difficulties. But Ranevskaya sees him as callous and totally indifferent to the misfortunes of others. He is shamelessly pestering her at such a terrible time in her life. Pishchik's action is to wear out Ranevskaya, to corner her. Ranevskaya's action is to avoid talking to him; it is useless to explain anything to him.

Hints: Pishchik is asking for money with all the familiarity of a close friend having no doubts that he will not be refused such a trifle.

Event 3.15 (Leading Character Dunyasha)

DUNYASHA: *[She has stopped to powder herself]* My young lady tells me to dance. There are plenty of gentlemen, and too few ladies, but dancing makes me giddy and makes my heart beat. Firs, the post-office clerk said something to me just now that quite took my breath away.
[Music becomes more subdued]
FIRS: What did he say to you?
DUNYASHA: He said I was like a flower.
YASHA: *[Yawns]* What ignorance.... *[Goes out]*
DUNYASHA: Like a flower.... I am a girl of such delicate feelings, I am awfully fond of soft speeches.
FIRS: Your head's being turned.

We considered this event earlier, in Part One. Today Dunyasha is enormously successful. Now Yasha, who has cooled toward her, can see her true worth.

Conflict between Dunyasha and Yasha and Firs: Dunyasha sees herself as a charming young lady, an object of male adoration. But to Yasha she is primarily a rustic servant of no interest whatsoever. Dunyasha thinks too highly of herself and is unduly boasting. For his part, Firs sees Dunyasha as a frivolous girl who has embarked on a slippery path. Worldly-wise Firs has seen much in his long life, and nothing in the house can escape his experienced eye. The true nature of the relationship between Dunyasha and Yasha is no secret to him.

Dunyasha's action is to stimulate Yasha's interest in her and make him jealous. Yasha's action is to put Dunyasha in her place. Firs's action is to forewarn and guide Dunyasha.

Hints: While speaking to Firs, Dunyasha is looking for Yasha's reaction to her words. Yasha is chewing something and watching the dancers. He does not look at Dunyasha. A tired Firs sits in the chair and listens attentively to Dunyasha.

Event 3.16 (Leading Character Epihodov)

[Enter Epihodov]

EPIHODOV: You have no desire to see me, Dunyasha.... It's as if I were some insect. *[Sighs]* Ah! life!

DUNYASHA: What is it you want?

EPIHODOV: Undoubtedly you may be right. *[Sighs]* But, of course, if one looks at it from that point of view, if I may so express myself, you have, excuse my plain speaking, reduced me to a complete state of mind. I know my destiny. Every day some misfortune befalls me and I have long ago grown accustomed to it, so that I look upon my fate with a smile. You gave me your word, and though I...

DUNYASHA: Please let us have a talk later, but now leave me in peace, for I am lost in reverie. *[Plays with her fan]*

EPIHODOV: I have a misfortune every day, and if I may venture to express myself, I merely smile at it, I even laugh.

Dunyasha no longer pays any attention to Epihodov. Conflict: Epihodov sees himself as a significant person who cannot simply be discounted. But to Dunyasha he is a fool who refuses to recognize that he has been rejected.

Epihodov's action is to startle. Dunyasha's action is to get rid of him.

Hints: Epihodov is speaking unhurriedly and impressively, enjoying his own speech. Dunyasha covers her face with a fan and turns away from Epihodov so that he cannot see her teary eyes.

Event 3.17 (Leading Character Varya)

[Varya enters from the larger drawing room]

VARYA: You still have not gone, Semyon? What a disrespectful creature you are, really. *[To Dunyasha]* Go along, Dunyasha! *[To Epihodov]* First you play billiards and break the cue, then you go wandering about the drawing room like a guest!

EPIHODOV: You really cannot, if I may so express myself, call me to account like this.

VARYA: I'm not calling you to account, I'm speaking to you. You do nothing but wander from place to place and you don't work. We keep you as a clerk, but what use you are I can't say.

EPIHODOV: *[Offended]* Whether I work or whether I walk, whether I eat or whether I play billiards, is a matter to be judged by persons of understanding and my elders.

VARYA: You dare to tell me that! *[Firing up]* You dare? You mean to say I've no understanding? Begone from here! This minute!

EPIHODOV: *[Intimidated]* I beg you to express yourself with delicacy.

VARYA: *[Beside herself with anger]* This moment! get out! away! *[He goes toward the door, she following him]* Two and twenty misfortunes! Take yourself off! Don't let me set eyes on you! *[Epihodov has gone out, behind the door his voice, "I shall complain about you"]* What! You're coming back? *[Snatches up the cane Firs put down near the door]* Come! Come! Come! I'll show you! What! you're coming? Then take that!

[She swings the cane, at the very moment that Lopahin comes in]

Epihodov has gotten out of hand. He has come uninvited to the ball, where he doesn't belong, and insists on staying despite Varya's orders. Conflict: Varya sees herself as the authoritative mistress of the house, whose orders Epihodov must obey. But to Epihodov she is a just a young girl with no authority over him. He is a respected person with a special position in the house. He is a clerk, not anyone's servant.

Varya's action is to subdue Epihodov, cut him down to size, force him to submit. The ultimate argument for her is a stick. Epihodov's action is to stand up for himself.

Hints: Varya gradually advances on Epihodov, but it makes no impression on him. He coolly coins his words, striking his pointing finger against the table top in rhythm.

Event 3.18 (Leading Character Lopahin)

LOPAHIN: Very much obliged to you!
VARYA: *[Angrily and ironically]* I beg your pardon!
LOPAHIN: Not at all. I humbly thank you for your kind reception.
VARYA: No need of thanks for it. *[Moves away, then looks round and asks softly]* I haven't hurt you?
LOPAHIN: Oh, no. Not at all. There's an immense bump coming up, though.

A funny thing happens with Lopahin: as the new owner of the house, he is greeted with a stick. Conflict: Lopahin believes he has every reason to be happy and to laugh. But to Varya he is a person whose jokes, as always, are ill-timed and out of place. Lopahin's jokes have long been irritating to Varya (E1.10, E2.19), but today, the sad day of the estate sale, they are especially inappropriate.

Lopahin's action is to arouse Varya's curiosity and make her share his joy. He clearly suggests to her that he deserves better treatment ("I humbly thank you for your kind reception"). Varya's action is not to support Lopahin and to change the subject.

Hints: Lopahin avoids Varya's gaze for fear of giving her, unintentionally, any hope.

Event 3.19 (Leading Character Ranevskaya)

VOICES FROM LARGER ROOM: Lopahin has come! Yermolay Alexeyevich!

PISHCHIK: What do I see and hear.... *[Kisses Lopahin]* There's a whiff of cognac about you, my dear soul. And we're making merry here too!

[Enter Ranevskaya]

RANEVSKAYA: Is it you, Yermolay Alexeyevich? Why have you been so long? Where's Leonid?

LOPAHIN: Leonid Andreyevich arrived with me. He is coming.

RANEVSKAYA: *[In agitation]* Well! Well! Was there a sale? Speak!

LOPAHIN: *[Embarrassed, afraid of betraying his joy]* The sale was over at four o'clock. We missed our train—had to wait till half-past nine. *[Sighing heavily]* Ugh! I feel a little giddy....

At last the torment of waiting is over, her brother and Lopahin have returned from the auction. Conflict: Ranevskaya sees Lopahin as a supporter, a person who shares her concerns. But Lopahin is far from Ranevskaya and her problems. For him now there is nothing but his remarkable success.

Ranevskaya's action is to wake up Lopahin, to pull at him. He is silent, as if he doesn't understand how much each minute of uncertainty is costing her. Lopahin's action is to avoid an answer. He feels uncomfortable telling Ranevskaya that he has bought her estate. He is waiting for Gaev to come in and tell everything himself.

Hints: Ranevskaya enters, expecting to find the recently arrived Gaev. Lopahin avoids Ranevskaya's gaze.

Event 3.20 (Leading Character Ranevskaya)

[Enter Gaev. In his right hand he has groceries, with his left he is wiping away his tears]

RANEVSKAYA: Well, Leonid, well? *[Impatiently, with tears]* Make haste, for God's sake....

GAEV: *[Makes no answer, simply waves his hand. To Firs, weeping]* Here, take them; there's anchovies, Kerch herrings. I have eaten nothing all day. What I have been through! *[Door into the billiard room is open. There is heard a knocking of balls and the voice of Yasha saying "Seven and eighteen!" Gaev's expression changes, he leaves off weeping]* I am fearfully tired. Firs, come and help me change my clothes. *[Goes to his room across the larger drawing room]*

Lopahin hesitates and doesn't say how the auction ended; Gaev weeps. Ranevskaya understands that the estate is gone. Conflict between Ranevskaya and Gaev: Gaev is the only person whom she needs and with whom she can share her tragedy. But Gaev considers himself to be ill-suited to offer comfort. He has suffered today as it is. Besides, Gaev considers it beneath his dignity to speak of the family's misfortune in the presence of the triumphant Lopahin.

Ranevskaya's action is to keep the company of her brother, whom she has been awaiting so impatiently all evening. Gaev's action is to avoid discussing the auction.

Hints: Ranevskaya runs toward her brother who walks by without stopping. Firs, mumbling, follows Gaev.

Event 3.21 (Leading Characters Ranevskaya and Pishchik)

PISHCHIK: How about the sale? Tell us, do!
RANEVSKAYA: Is the cherry orchard sold?
LOPAHIN: It is sold.
RANEVSKAYA: Who has bought it?
LOPAHIN: I have bought it. *[A pause]*
[Ranevskaya is crushed; she would fall down if she were not standing near a chair and table. Varya takes keys from her waistband, flings them on the floor in the middle of the drawing room, and goes out]

It is clear to everyone that the estate is lost. But Gaev has not announced any specifics, and Lopahin has remained quiet. Conflict: Ranevskaya and Pishchik perceive Lopahin as a humane person who is sparing Ranevskaya from being wounded. But he is completely engrossed by his success.

Pishchik and Ranevskaya's action is to give Lopahin a starting push. Lopahin's action is to prolong the time before answering, and to remain aloof. He tries to restrain his joy.

Hints: Pishchik pushes Lopahin to speak. Ranevskaya is leaning back, supporting herself with her hands on the edge of the table. She looks at Lopahin who continues to avoid her gaze.

Event 3.22 (Leading Character Lopahin)

LOPAHIN: I have bought it! Wait a bit, ladies and gentlemen, pray. My head's a bit muddled, I can't speak.... *[Laughs]* We came to the auction. Deriganov was there already. Leonid Andreyevich only had fifteen thousands and Deriganov bid thirty thousands besides the arrears, straight off. I saw how the land lay. I bid against him. I bid forty, he bid forty-five, I said fifty-five, and so he went on, adding five thousands and I adding ten.... Well, so it ended. I bid ninety, and it was knocked down to me. Now the cherry orchard's mine! Mine! *[Laughs]* My God, the cherry orchard's mine! Tell me that I'm drunk, that I'm out of my mind, that it's all a dream.... *[Stamps with his feet]* Don't laugh at me! If my father and my grandfather could rise from their grave and see all that has happened. How their Yermolay, ignorant, beaten Yermolay, who used to run about barefoot in winter, how that very Yermolay has bought the finest estate in the world. I have bought the estate where my father and grandfather were slaves, where they weren't even admitted into the kitchen. I am asleep, I am dreaming.... It is all fancy, it is the work of your imagination plunged in the darkness of uncertainty.... *[Picks up the keys, smiling fondly]* She threw away the keys; she means to show she's not the mistress here any more. *[Jingles the keys]* Well, no matter. *[The orchestra is heard tuning up]* Hey, musicians! Play! I want to hear you! Come, all of you, and look how Yermolay Lopahin will take the axe to the cherry orchard, how the trees will fall to the ground! We will build houses on it and our grandsons and great-grandsons will see a new life springing up there. Music! Play up!

[*Music begins to play. Ranevskaya has sunk into a chair and is weeping bitterly*]

Finally everyone knows that Lopahin has bought the estate. He is no longer able to hold back the joy surging in him: the son of an illiterate peasant has gotten the upper hand over the wealthy Deriganov and purchased the estate. Conflict between Lopahin and Ranevskaya: Lopahin sees himself as a victor, winning everyone's respect and admiration. But to Ranevskaya he is a vulgar person who has forgotten himself: Lopahin loudly rejoices at his success in the presence of Ranevskaya when this terrible misfortune has befallen her family.

Lopahin's action is to glorify himself. Ranevskaya's action is to ignore his presence.

Hints: Since Ranevskaya has isolated herself from Lopahin, he directs his speech to Pishchik, who is listening to him with admiration. After accidentally stepping on a set of keys thrown by Varya, Lopahin tenderly picks them up, and then jingles them, enjoying their quiet ringing. He is slightly tipsy (see E3.19).

Event 3.23 (Leading Character Lopahin)

LOPAHIN: [*Reproachfully*] Why, why didn't you listen to me? My poor, my dear lady, there's no turning back now. [*With tears*] Oh, if all this could be over, if our unhappy disjointed life could somehow soon be changed.

Lopahin sees Ranevskaya's weeping as a reproach, an accusation of his having done something unseemly. Conflict: Lopahin considers himself blameless with regard to Ranevskaya. But to her he is an ill-mannered boor. He has just loudly boasted how he will cut down her beloved orchard.

Lopahin's action is to justify and defend himself against unfair accusations. He has nothing to be ashamed of: all these months he has been trying to help Ranevskaya; had she heeded him, she would now have nothing to grieve about. Ranevskaya's action is to ignore Lopahin.

Hints: Lopahin kneels on one knee before Ranevskaya, kisses her hand, and looks into her eyes.

Event 3.24 (Leading Character Pishchik)

PISHCHIK: *[Takes him by the arm, in an undertone]* She's weeping. Let us go and leave her alone.... Come.... *[Takes him by the arm and leads him into the larger drawing room]*

LOPAHIN: What's that? Musicians, play up! All must be as I wish it! *[With irony]* Here comes the new master, the owner of the cherry orchard! *[Accidentally tips over a little table, almost upsetting the candelabra]* I can pay for everything! *[Goes out with Pishchik]*

Lopahin is drunk; he has lost his head and doesn't understand Ranevskaya's state of mind. Conflict: Pishchik considers that Lopahin has lost all sense of tact. But Lopahin sees himself as person who has every right openly to celebrate his success. Today is his day. Pishchik's action is to quiet Lopahin. Lopahin's action is to insist on his right to celebrate.

Hints: See author's stage directions.

Event 3.25 (Leading Character Anya)

[No one remains on the stage or in the larger drawing room except Ranevskaya, who sits huddled up, weeping bitterly. The music plays softly. Anya and Trofimov come in quickly. Anya goes up to her mother and falls on her knees before her. Trofimov stands at the entrance to the larger drawing room]

ANYA: Mamma!... Mamma, you're crying? Dear, kind, my good mamma, my precious mamma, I love you... I bless you. The cherry orchard is sold, it is gone, that's true, that's true. But don't weep, mamma; life is still before you, you have still your good, pure heart.... Let us go, let us go, darling, away from here!... We will make a new garden, more splendid than this one; you will see it, you will understand. And joy, quiet, deep joy, will sink into your soul like the sun at evening, and you will smile, mamma! Come, darling, let us go!...

Mamma doesn't understand that nothing terrible has happened, that a new and interesting life lies ahead for her. Conflict: Anya sees herself as her mother's mentor and guide. But to Ranevskaya she is a child with no knowledge of life. Anya is incapable of understanding the misfortune that has befallen her family.

Anya's action is to guide and lead her mother, using the words of Petya Trofimov. Ranevskaya's action is to avoid any discussions. She has no wish to destroy Anya's illusions.

Hints: Ranevskaya embraces Anya and strokes her hair. Trofimov makes no attempt to approach Ranevskaya.

21. Act IV

The same as Act I. There are neither curtains on the windows nor pictures on the walls. Only a few pieces of furniture remain piled in a corner, as if for sale. There is a sense of emptiness. Near the outer door and in the background of the scene are packed trunks, traveling bags, and so forth. On the left the door is open, and from here the voices of Varya and Anya are heard. Lopahin is standing waiting. Yasha is holding a tray with glasses of champagne. In the anteroom Epihodov is tying up a box. In the background behind the scene a hum of talk from the peasants who have come to say goodbye. The voice of Gaev: "Thanks, brothers, thanks."

Event 4.1 (Leading Character Yasha)

YASHA: The peasants have come to say goodbye. In my

138

opinion, Yermolay Alexeyevich, the peasants are good-natured, but they don't know much about things.

[*The hum of talk dies away. Enter across front of stage Ranevskaya and Gaev. She is not weeping but is pale; her face is quivering—she cannot speak*]

GAEV: You gave them your purse, Lyuba. That won't do! That won't do!

RANEVSKAYA: I couldn't help it! I couldn't help it! [*Both go out*]

LOPAHIN: [*In the doorway, calls after them*] Please take a glass at parting! Please do! I didn't think to bring any from the town, and at the station I could only get one bottle. Please take a glass! [*A pause*] Well, you don't care for any? [*Comes away from the door*] If I'd known, I wouldn't have bought it. Well, and I'm not going to drink it. [*Yasha carefully sets the tray down on a chair*] You have a glass, Yasha, anyway.

YASHA: Good luck to the travelers, and luck to those that stay behind! [*Drinks*] This champagne isn't the real thing, I can assure you.

LOPAHIN: It cost eight rubles a bottle. [*A pause*] It's devilish cold here.

YASHA: They haven't heated the stove today—it's all the same since we're going. [*Laughs*]

LOPAHIN: What are you laughing for?

YASHA: For pleasure.

LOPAHIN: Though it's October, it's as still and sunny as though it were summer. It's just right for building. [*Looks at his watch; says in doorway*] Take note, ladies and gentlemen, the train goes in forty-seven minutes! So you ought to start for the station in twenty minutes. Hurry up.

In his mind's eye, Yasha is already in Paris. Conflict between Yasha and Lopahin: Yasha sees himself as a European with nothing in common with these people or these parts. But to Lopahin he is a worthless valet, unworthy of attention.

Yasha's action is to show his superiority over the uncouth Lopahin who has no idea of civilized life. Lopahin's action is to keep Yasha at arm's length. Note that just a few months ago Lopahin was shaking Yasha's hand as an equal (E1.29).

In this event there is also an incidental conflict between Lopahin (leading character) and Gaev and Ranevskaya. After Lopahin's purchase of the estate, the others have taken offense (E3.23); they refuse to talk and generally ignore him. But Lopahin is above petty offense, and today he has come especially to bid the Ranevskaya family farewell. Conflict: Lopahin sees himself as being close to Ranevskaya's family, as a friend of the house. But to them he is a vulgar person who has forgotten who he is. He invites them to celebrate with champagne what is a tragic event in their life: parting with their family estate.

Lopahin's action is to make up and establish good relations. Ranevskaya's and Gaev's action is to ignore his presence. For them he does not exist.

Hints: Yasha is ready to leave, traveling cap on his head and a scarf around his neck. He keeps trying to get Lopahin to notice him, but Lopahin's attention is turned toward Ranevskaya and Gaev.

Event 4.2 (Leading Character Lopahin)

[Trofimov, in an overcoat, comes in from the outside]

TROFIMOV: I think it must be time to start, the horses are ready. The devil only knows what's become of my galoshes. They're lost. *[In the doorway]* Anya! My galoshes aren't here. I can't find them!

LOPAHIN: And I'm getting off to Kharkov. I am going in the same train with you. I'm spending all the winter in Kharkov. I've been hanging around with you and fretting with no work to do. I can't get on without work. I don't know what to do with my hands, they flap about so queerly, as if they didn't belong to me.

TROFIMOV: Well, we're just going away, and you will take up your useful labors again.

LOPAHIN: Do take a glass.

TROFIMOV: No, thanks.

Analysis of The Cherry Orchard

LOPAHIN: Then you're going to Moscow now?
TROFIMOV: Yes. I shall see them as far as the town, and tomorrow I shall go on to Moscow.
LOPAHIN: Yes.... The professors must be giving no lectures, they're waiting for your arrival.
TROFIMOV: That's not your business.
LOPAHIN: How many years have you been at the University?
TROFIMOV: Do think of something new. That's stale and flat. *[Looking for his galoshes]* You know we shall most likely never see each other again, so let me give you one piece of advice at parting: don't wave your arms about—get out of the habit. And building summer cottages, reckoning up that the summer residents will in time become independent farmers—reckoning like that is also a sort of arm-waving.... After all, I like you all the same. You have fine delicate fingers like an artist, you've a fine delicate soul....

Like Ranevskaya and Gaev, Trofimov ignores Lopahin. Conflict: Lopahin considers himself an old friend of the student Trofimov whom he has known for many years. But Trofimov sees him as a person who is alien in spirit and with whom he can have nothing in common. The self-confident, tactless Lopahin sickens Trofimov.

Lopahin's action is to win over Trofimov and part in good faith. In his efforts to establish better relations, he repeats the same jokes that earlier brought them into confrontation (see E2.11). Trofimov's action is to shun all attempts at reconciliation. As in E2.11, Trofimov first tries to get rid of Lopahin, then, when he sees this is impossible, he cruelly ridicules him. To understand Trofimov's sarcasm—"you have fine delicate fingers like an artist, you've a fine delicate soul"—it should be recalled that Trofimov earlier compared Lopahin to an all-devouring predator and, like Gaev, sees him as a money-grubber capable only of filling his pockets.

Hints: Lopahin brings Trofimov a glass of champagne. Trofimov is totally immersed in the search for his galoshes; in passing he converses with Lopahin without looking at him.

Event 4.3 (Leading Character Lopahin)

LOPAHIN: *[Embraces him]* Goodbye, my dear fellow. Thanks for everything. Let me give you money for the journey, if you need it.

TROFIMOV: What for? I don't need it.

LOPAHIN: But you don't have any!

TROFIMOV: Yes, I have, thank you. I got some money for a translation. Here it is in my pocket. *[Anxiously]* But where can my galoshes be!

VARYA: *[From the next room]* Take the nasty things!

[Flings a pair of galoshes on the stage]

TROFIMOV: Why are you so cross, Varya? H'mm...but those aren't my galoshes!

LOPAHIN: I sowed three thousand acres with poppies in the spring, and now I have cleared forty thousand profit. And when my poppies were in flower, wasn't it a picture! So here, as I say, I made forty thousand, and I am offering you a loan because I can afford to. Why turn up your nose? I am a peasant—I speak bluntly.

TROFIMOV: Your father was a peasant, mine was a druggist—and that proves absolutely nothing whatever. *[Lopahin takes out his wallet]* Stop that, stop that.... If you were to offer me two hundred thousand I wouldn't take it. I am a free man, and everything that all of you, rich and poor alike, prize so highly and hold so dear, hasn't the slightest power over me—it's like so much fluff fluttering in the air. I can get on without you, I can pass by you. I am strong and proud. Humanity is advancing toward the highest truth, the highest happiness which is possible on earth, and I am in the front ranks!

LOPAHIN: Will you get there?

TROFIMOV: I shall get there. *[A pause]* I shall get there, or I shall show others the way to get there.

[In the distance is heard the stroke of an axe on a tree]

LOPAHIN: Goodbye, my dear fellow. It's time to be off. We turn up our noses at one another, but life is passing all the while. When I am working hard without resting, then my mind is more at ease, and it seems to me as though I too know what I exist for. But how many people are in Russia, my friend, who exist, one doesn't know what for. Well, it doesn't matter, that's not what keeps things spinning. They tell that Leonid Andreyevich has taken a position at the bank—six thousand a year.... Only, of course, he won't stick to it—he's too lazy....

In response to Lopahin's friendly overtures, Trofimov snubs him and openly demonstrates his dislike. Conflict: Lopahin sees Trofimov as a miserable ne'er-do-well who has nothing to his credit but high-blown rhetoric. But Trofimov considers himself strong and independent, towering over the world of the Lopahins. He has devoted his life not to senseless money-grubbing but to serving others.

Lopahin's action is to expose Trofimov's worthlessness. As proof that he is right, Lopahin shows off a wallet filled with money and lumps Trofimov together with that do-nothing babbler Gaev. Now Lopahin even flaunts the fact that he is a peasant (compare with his monologue in E1.2). Varya joins Lopahin and offers one more proof of Trofimov's worthlessness: his only possession is a pair of old, worn galoshes.

Trofimov's action is to defend himself and his character. Unlike Lopahin, who is a pauper in spirit, he is free from the power of money and has a noble purpose in life.

Hints: Lopahin, with an exaggerated grand gesture, embraces Trofimov who is trying to free himself, and then unhurriedly takes out and opens his wallet.

Event 4.4 (Leading Characters Anya and Trofimov)

ANYA: *[In the doorway]* Mamma asks you not to cut down the orchard until she's gone.

TROFIMOV: Really, you might have the tact...*[Goes out through the anteroom]*

LOPAHIN: At once, at once.... What people, really.
[Goes out after him]

Lopahin has gone too far: he has begun to cut down Ranevskaya's beloved cherry orchard in her presence. Conflict: Anya and Trofimov see Lopahin as a boor with no concern for anything but his own selfish interests. But Lopahin considers himself above reproach in his attitude toward Ranevskaya and her family. He has come especially to bid them all farewell. As for cutting down the orchard, does it really matter whether to start now or in half an hour?

Anya's and Trofimov's action is to bring Lopahin in line. Lopahin's action is to yield to these "strange people" (see E2.6).

Hints: Trofimov is only too happy to sting Lopahin. Perplexed, Lopahin spreads his hands in a helpless gesture, wondering what everyone wants of him.

Event 4.5 (Leading Character Anya)

ANYA: Has Firs been taken to the hospital?

YASHA: I told them this morning. No doubt they have taken him.

ANYA: *[To Epihodov, who passes across the room]* Semyon Panteleyevich, inquire, please, if Firs has been taken to the hospital.

YASHA: *[In a tone of offense]* I told Yegor this morning— why ask a dozen times!

EPIHODOV: Firs is advanced in years. It's my conclusive opinion no treatment would do him good; it's time he was gathered to his fathers. And I can only envy him. *[Puts a suitcase on a hatbox and crushes it]* There, now, of course— I knew it would be so. *[Goes out]*

YASHA: *[Mockingly]* Two and twenty misfortunes....

Mamma and uncle are distraught and incapable of dealing with the business of moving out. Conflict: Anya sees herself as a mistress of the house as much as Varya. But to Yasha and Epihodov, she is just a young girl with no real authority. All the more so as they are no longer bound to this house.

144

Anya's action is to supervise the servants and make them do their jobs. Yasha's action is to shirk his duties. Yasha's noisy indignation at the distrust displayed toward him dismays Anya, who naively takes his words at face value (see E4.13). Epihodov now has a new boss—Lopahin—and he simply ignores Anya's orders.

Hints: Anya's orders tear Yasha away from enjoying an expensive champagne.

Event 4.6 (Leading Character Varya)

VARYA: *[Through the door]* Has Firs been taken to the hospital?
ANYA: Yes.
VARYA: Why wasn't the letter to the doctor taken too?
ANYA: Then, we must send it after them.... *[Goes out]*

Anya has intervened unasked in domestic affairs. Varya sees her as a person who cannot be relied upon, but Anya considers herself to be as good as Varya. She holds the same position in the house and is capable of dealing with everything. Varya's action is to keep everything under her control. Anya's action is to stand on her own.

Hints: Varya peeks out of the door and hands Anya a letter.

Event 4.7 (Leading Character Varya)

VARYA: *[From the adjoining room]* Where's Yasha? Tell him his mother's come to say goodbye to him.
YASHA: *[Waves his hand]* They put me out of all patience. *[Dunyasha has all this time been bustling about the luggage. Now, when Yasha is left alone, she goes up to him]*

Yasha is again behaving shamefully, refusing to say goodbye to his mother. Conflict: Varya considers herself responsible for everything in the house. But Yasha considers her no longer relevant. He is leaving for Paris. Varya's action is the same as in the preceding event, namely, to keep everything under control. Yasha's action is to avoid talking with Varya. He prefers to say nothing.

Hints: Yasha, standing by the window, thievishly drinks champagne.

Event 4.8 (Leading Character Dunyasha)

DUNYASHA: You might just give me one look, Yasha. You're going away.... You're leaving me.... *[Weeps and throws herself on his neck]*

YASHA: What are you crying for? *[Drinks the champagne]* In six days I shall be in Paris again. Tomorrow we shall get into the express train and roll away in a flash. I can scarcely believe it. Vive la France!... It doesn't suit me here—it's not the life for me.... There's no doing anything. I have seen enough of the ignorance here. I have had enough of it. *[Drinks champagne]* What are you crying for? Behave yourself properly, and then you won't cry.

DUNYASHA: *[Powders her face, looking in her mirror]* Do send me a letter from Paris. You know how I loved you, Yasha—how I loved you! I am a tender creature, Yasha!

YASHA: Here they are coming. *[Bustles about the trunks, humming softly]*

Yasha, who is leaving, pays Dunyasha no attention and does not even say goodbye to her. Conflict: Dunyasha perceives herself to be a tender and sensitive young lady deserving delicate treatment, but to Yasha she is only a peasant servant with whom one need not stand on ceremony. Their passing intrigue is over without leaving Yasha any memories. Dunyasha's action is to part as a real lady would. Yasha's action is to distance himself from Dunyasha, not to take part in her theatrics.

Hints: Dunyasha puts on a parting act (see author's stage directions). Yasha pleasurably finishes the last glass of champagne.

Event 4.9 (Leading Character Anya)

[*Enter Ranevskaya, Gaev, Anya, and Charlotta Ivanovna*]
GAEV: We ought to be off. There's not much time now. [*Looking at Yasha*] What a smell of herrings!

RANEVSKAYA: In ten minutes we must get into the carriage. [*Casts a look about the room*] Farewell, dear house, dear old grandfather. Winter will pass and spring will come, and then you will be no more; they will tear you down. How much those walls have seen! [*Kisses her daughter passionately*] My treasure, how bright you look. Your eyes are sparkling like diamonds. Are you glad? Very glad?

ANYA: Very glad! A new life is beginning, mamma!

GAEV: Yes, really, everything is all right now. Before the cherry orchard was sold, we were all worried and wretched, but afterward, when once the question was settled conclusively, irrevocably, we all felt calm and even cheerful.... I am at the bank, I am a financier now...yellow to the side pocket. And you, Lyuba, after all, you are looking better; there's no question of that.

RANEVSKAYA: Yes. My nerves are better, that's true. [*Her hat and coat are handed to her*] I'm sleeping well. Carry out my things, Yasha. It's time. [*To Anya*] My darling, we shall soon see each other again.... I am going to Paris, and I'll live there on the money your Yaroslavl aunt sent us to buy the estate with—hurrah for aunt!—but that money won't last long.

ANYA: You'll come back soon, mamma, won't you? I'll be working up for my examination in the high school, and when I have passed that, I shall set to work and be a help to you. We will read all sort of things together, mamma, won't we? [*Kisses her mother's hands*] We will read lots of books, and a new wonderful world will open out before us.... [*Dreamily*] Mamma, come back....

RANEVSKAYA: I shall come, my precious treasure. [*Embraces her*]

Anya is delighted: at last the old life is over. Conflict between Anya and group comprising Gaev and Ranevskaya.

Anya sees herself at the threshold of a new and interesting life. But to her mother and uncle she is a child incapable of grasping the extent of their misfortune. Anya's action is to cheer her mother and uncle, to guide and lead them. Their action is to "play her game" and not destroy her illusions.

Hints: Ranevskaya, scarcely containing herself, crumples her handkerchief. Gaev, next to Ranevskaya at all times, tries to support her.

Event 4.10 (Leading Character Gaev)

> *[Enter Lopahin. Charlotta softly hums a song]*
> GAEV: Charlotta's happy: she's singing!
> CHARLOTTA: *[Picks up a bundle like a swaddled baby]* Bye, bye, my baby. *[A baby is heard crying: "Ooah! ooah!"]* Hush, hush, my pretty boy! *[Ooah! ooah!]* Poor little thing! *[Throws the bundle back]* You must please find me a position. I can't go on like this.
> LOPAHIN: We'll find you one, Charlotta Ivanovna. Don't you worry yourself.
> GAEV: Everyone's leaving us. Varya's going away.... We have become of no use all at once.
> CHARLOTTA: I don't have a place to live in town. I must go away.... *[Hums]* It doesn't matter....

Charlotta has asked Gaev to find a new position for her: she has decided to part with their family. Conflict between Gaev and Charlotta: Gaev sees himself as the master of the house whose duty it is to preserve the family. But Charlotta sees him as a ridiculous person who refuses to reckon with reality. The house no longer offers Charlotta either shelter or work, and she is compelled to start her life anew. Gaev's action is to reason with Charlotta and induce her to stay. Charlotta's action is to point out the hopelessness of her situation.

Incidental conflict between Lopahin and Charlotta: Lopahin thinks he can do anything. But Charlotta thinks he is butting into affairs that do not concern him. Only her employers can recommend her to another home. Lopahin's action is to remind Charlotta who he is. Charlotta ignores Lopahin.

Hints: See author's stage directions.

Event 4.11 (Leading Character Pishchik)

[Enter Pishchik]

LOPAHIN: The miracle of nature!

PISHCHIK: *[Gasping]* Oh...let me get my breath.... I'm worn out...my most honored.... Give me some water....

GAEV: Want some money, I suppose? Your humble servant! I'll go out of the way of temptation.... *[Goes out]*

PISHCHIK: It's a long while since I have been to see you... dearest lady. *[To Lopahin]* You are here...glad to see you...a man of immense intellect...take...here... *[Gives Lopahin money]* Four hundred rubles.... That leaves me owing eight hundred and forty.

LOPAHIN: *[Shrugging his shoulders in amazement]* It's like a dream.... Where did you get it?

PISHCHIK: Wait a bit...I'm hot.... A most extraordinary occurrence. Some Englishmen came along and found in my land some sort of white clay.... *[To Ranevskaya]* And four hundred for you...most lovely...wonderful.... *[Gives money]* The rest later. *[Drinks water]* A young man in the train was telling me just now that a great philosopher advises jumping off a roof.... "Jump!" says he; "the whole gist of the problem lies in that." *[Wonderingly]* Fancy that, now! Water, please!...

LOPAHIN: What Englishmen?

PISHCHIK: I have made over to them the rights to dig the clay for twenty-four years.... And now, excuse me.... I can't stay.... I must be galloping on.... I'm going to Znoikov...to Kardamonov.... I'm in debt all round.... *[Drinks]* Goodbye. I'll come in on Thursday....

RANEVSKAYA: We are just off to the town, and tomorrow I go abroad....

Pishchik is quite overcome by the turn of events in his life; besides, he hasn't visited with old friends for quite some time. Conflict between Pishchik and Gaev, Lopahin and Ranevskaya: Pishchik considers himself to be a welcome friend in the house, whose arrival is always greeted with pleasure. But to the others he is a person prone to freak escapades. He doesn't even realize that the estate has been sold nor sense the air of departure in the house.

Pishchik's action is to share his joy with his friends. Gaev's action is to remain aloof. His last minutes of parting with the house have come, and he has no use for Pishchik now. Lopahin's action is to amuse himself and poke fun at Pishchik. Ranevskaya's action is to calm Pishchik and bring him to his senses.

Hints: Pishchik broadly embraces Lopahin and kisses Ranevskaya's hands profusely. Like a magician, he takes out a wallet and hands out money. He delivers his news as if it were a miracle. Lopahin watches this performance with great pleasure. Gaev runs away from Pishchik. Ranevskaya sits motionless, her gaze wandering about the empty room.

Event 4.12 (Leading Character Pishchik)

PISHCHIK: What? *[In agitation]* Why to the town? Oh, I see the furniture...the luggage.... No matter.... *[Through his tears]* No matter.... Men of enormous intellect...these Englishmen.... Never mind...be happy...God will help you.... No matter.... Everything in this world must have an end.... *[Kisses Lyubov Andreyevna's hand]* If the rumor reaches you that my end has come, think of this...old horse, and say: "There once was such a man in the world...Semyonov-Pishchik...the Kingdom of Heaven be his."... Most extraordinary weather.... Yes.... *[Goes out in violent agitation, but at once returns and says in doorway]* Dashenka sends her love to you! *[Goes out]*

Pishchik finds himself in an awkward situation—in the midst of his own concerns he has forgotten that Ranevskaya has lost her estate. Conflict between Pishchik and Ranevskaya: He considers himself a devoted friend of the family, and parting with Ranevskaya is a sad occasion. But Ranevskaya sees him as a man uncaring of everyone except himself. Pishchik has always been indifferent to the troubles of other people (see E1.31, E1.36, E3.14), and nothing better can be expected of him.

Pishchik's action is to apologize, smooth over the unpleasant situation, and beg forgiveness. Ranevskaya's action is to ignore Pishchik. She does not believe his repentance is sincere.

Hints: Pishchik looks around the empty room, sees the baggage, and realizes what is happening. Seeing that he has shamed himself, Pishchik uneasily stomps his feet in place, mumbles, and, not knowing what to do, leaves.

Event 4.13 (Leading Character Ranevskaya)

RANEVSKAYA: Now we can go. I leave with two cares in my heart. The first is leaving Firs ill. *[Looking at her watch]* We have still five minutes.

ANYA: Mamma, Firs has been taken to the hospital. Yasha sent him off this morning.

RANEVSKAYA: My next anxiety is Varya. She is used to getting up early and working; and now, without work, she's like a fish out of water. She is thin and pale, and she's crying, poor thing....*[A pause]* You are well aware, Yermolay Alexeyevich, I dreamed of...marrying her to you, and everything seemed to show that you would get married. *[Whispers to Anya, she nods to Charlotta and both go out]* She loves you, you like her, and I don't know—I don't know why it is you seem, as it were, to avoid each other. I don't understand it!

LOPAHIN: I don't understand it myself, I confess. It's strange somehow, altogether.... If there's still time, I'm ready now at once.... Let's settle it once and for all; but without you, I feel I shall not propose to her.

RANEVSKAYA: That's excellent. Why, a single minute's all that's necessary. I'll call her at once....

LOPAHIN: And there's champagne all ready, too. *[Looking into the glasses]* They're empty, someone has drunk them already. *[Yasha coughs]* It's called, swilled them....

RANEVSKAYA: *[Eagerly]* Excellent. We will go out.... Yasha allez! I'll call her in.... *[At the door]* Varya, leave all that; come here. Come along! *[Goes out with Yasha]*

Lopahin has let Ranevskaya down: he promised to marry Varya and has not proposed. Conflict: Ranevskaya considers Lopahin's behavior toward her family to be unworthy. But Lopahin sees himself as blameless, a gentleman. He loves Ranevskaya and does his best for this family. And though he did think about marrying Varya, he has never given her ground for such hopes.

Ranevskaya's action is to press Lopahin and to corner him. Lopahin's action is to cleanse and repair their relationship. He is troubled by these unexpected reproaches.

Hints: Ranevskaya looks long and hard into Lopahin's eyes. Lopahin, completely lost, not realizing what he says or does, grabs the bottle and the glasses, ready to do anything to please Ranevskaya.

Event 4.14 (Leading Character Lopahin)

LOPAHIN: *[Looking at his watch]* Yes....

[A pause. Behind the door, restrained laughter and whispering, and, at last, Varya enters]

VARYA: *[Looking a long while over the things]* It is strange, I can't find it anywhere....

LOPAHIN: What are you looking for?

VARYA: I packed it myself, and I can't remember. *[A pause]*

LOPAHIN: Where are you going now, Varvara Mihailovna?

VARYA: I? To the Rogulins.... I have arranged to go to them to look after the house...a housekeeper, kind of.

LOPAHIN: That's in Yashnovo? It'll be about fifty miles away. *[A pause]* So this is the end of life in this house....

VARYA: *[Looking among the things]* Where is it.... Perhaps I put it in the trunk.... Yes, life in this house is over—there will be no more of it....

LOPAHIN: And I'm just off to Kharkov...by this next train. I've a lot of business there. I'm leaving Epihodov here, and I've hired him.

VARYA: Why not!

LOPAHIN: This time last year we had snow already, if you remember; but now it's so fine and sunny. Though it's cold... twenty-seven degrees, perhaps.

VARYA: I haven't looked. *[A pause]* And besides, our thermometer's broken.... *[A pause]*

[Voice at the door from the yard: "Yermolay Alexeyevich!"]

LOPAHIN: *[As though he had long been expecting this summons]* This minute!

[Lopahin goes out quickly. Varya, sitting on the floor and laying her head on a bag full of clothes, sobs quietly.]

Lopahin understands he has made a mistake by yielding to Ranevskaya's influence: he has other plans in life in which there is no place for Varya. Conflict: Lopahin considers himself independent and capable of deciding his own fate. But Varya sees him as following Ranevskaya's lead. Varya, who has long since abandoned any hope of marriage, can't believe that Lopahin has decided to propose to her on his own.

Lopahin's action is to define their relationship and indicate to Varya that she should not count on him. He greets Varya with a long pause, then asks about her plans for the future (taken aback by the question, Varya even asks him to repeat it). Lopahin then goes on to inform her that he is leaving shortly, after which the conversation shifts to the weather. Varya's action is to wait, which she does by pretending to be preoccupied with household affairs.

Hints: Lopahin checks his watch and walks to the window, his back toward entering Varya. He passes the time expecting to be summoned at any moment.

Event 4.15 (Leading Character Ranevskaya)

[Ranevskaya comes in cautiously]

RANEVSKAYA: Well? *[A pause]* We must be going.

VARYA: *[Has wiped her eyes and is no longer crying]* Yes, mamma, it's time. I shall have time to get to the Rogulins today, if only we're not late for the train....

Varya is in despair because Lopahin has failed to propose to her. Conflict: Ranevskaya sees herself as a person whose help is especially important for Varya at this point. But Varya considers that Ranevskaya is intruding into something of no concern to her. She is trying to arrange Varya's fate without ever having really understood either her life or her relationship with Lopahin.

Ranevskaya's action is to help and support Varya. Varya's action is to sidestep explanations.

Hints: After entering, Ranevskaya looks for Lopahin and understands the situation.

Event 4.16 (Leading Character Gaev)

RANEVSKAYA: *[In the doorway]* Anya, put your things on!
[Enter Anya, then Gaev and Charlotta. Gaev has on a warm coat with a hood. Servants and cabmen come in. Epihodov bustles about the luggage]
RANEVSKAYA: Now we can start on our travels.
ANYA: *[Joyfully]* On our travels!
GAEV: My friends—my dear, my precious friends! Leaving this house forever, can I be silent? Can I refrain myself from expressing at leave-taking those emotions which now flood all my being....
ANYA: *[Supplicatingly]* Uncle!
VARYA: Uncle, don't!
GAEV: *[Dejectedly]* Yellow to the side pocket.... I'll be quiet....

The time has come to bid farewell to the house. But no one seems to grasp the tragedy of the moment. Conflict between Gaev and his nieces: Gaev sees himself as the head of the family on whose shoulders lies the sad duty of uttering the parting words before the family leaves their house forever.

Analysis of The Cherry Orchard

But Anya and Varya consider Gaev an inveterate babbler.

Gaev's action is to gather and unite the family. Anya's and Varya's action is to put an end to their uncle's useless tirades.

Hints: Gaev begins his speech with unusual ceremony.

Event 4.17 (Leading Character Lopahin)

[Enter Trofimov and afterward Lopahin]

TROFIMOV: Well, ladies and gentlemen, we must start!

LOPAHIN: Epihodov, my coat!

RANEVSKAYA: I'll stay one more minute. It seems as though I have never seen before what the walls, what the ceilings in this house were like, and now I look at them with greediness, with such tender love....

GAEV: I remember when I was six years old sitting in this window on Trinity Day watching my father going to the church....

RANEVSKAYA: Have all the things been taken?

LOPAHIN: It seems that's all. *[Putting on overcoat, to Epihodov]* You, Epihodov, mind you see everything is right.

EPIHODOV: *[In a husky voice]* Don't worry, Yermolay Alexeyevich!

LOPAHIN: Why, what's wrong with your voice?

EPIHODOV: I've just drunk some water and swallowed something.

YASHA: *[Contemptuously]* The ignorance....

RANEVSKAYA: We are going—and not a soul will be left here....

LOPAHIN: Not till the spring.

VARYA: *[Pulls an umbrella out of a bundle, as though to hit someone with it. Lopahin pretends to be frightened]* Why...I didn't mean anything.

TROFIMOV: Ladies and gentlemen, let us get into the carriages.... It's time! The train will be in shortly!

VARYA: Petya, here they are, your galoshes, by the box. *[With tears]* And what dirty old things they are....

TROFIMOV: *[Putting on his galoshes]* Let us go, ladies and gentlemen!

155

GAEV: *[Greatly embarrassed, afraid of weeping]* The train... the station.... Bank off the cushion, white to the corner....

RANEVSKAYA: Let us go!

LOPAHIN: Everybody is here? Nobody is there? *[Locks the side door on left]* The things are all here. We must lock up. Let us go!

ANYA: Goodbye, home! Goodbye, old life!

TROFIMOV: Welcome to the new life! *[Goes out with Anya]*

[Varya looks round the room and goes out slowly. Yasha and Charlotta, with her dog, go out]

LOPAHIN: Till the spring now. Come, ladies and gentlemen.... Goodbye! *[Goes out]*

There is nothing left to bind Lopahin with Ranevskaya after he has failed to propose to Varya, and he is parting for good with the family that never really understood him.

Conflict between Lopahin and a group comprising Ranevskaya and Gaev: Lopahin sees himself as an important person, the new master of life, well aware of his worth. But to Ranevskaya and Gaev he is a person who does not deserve their attention.

Lopahin's action is to impress on them who he is. He highhandedly demands to be given his coat, mentions twice that his great plan will be implemented next spring, and leaves with scarcely a farewell. He doesn't care what they may think of him and even jokes about not having proposed to Varya (scene with the umbrella).

Ranevskaya's and Gaev's action is to isolate themselves from Lopahin. They neither see nor hear him, though he keeps intruding and interfering with them as they say farewell to the house.

In this event there are two incidental conflicts: Trofimov (Leading Character) with Ranevskaya, Gaev, and Varya; and Epihodov (Leading Character) with Yasha.

Trofimov's efforts have not been in vain: Anya has accepted

his ideas and parts with her old life without regrets. Trofimov sees himself as a leader in steering the Ranevskaya family toward a new life. But to Ranevskaya and Gaev he is a meddling intruder. Varya, for her part, sees him as a nonentity.

Trofimov's action is to guide and lead. He is joined by Anya. Ranevskaya and Gaev simply pay no attention to him. Varya's action is to bring Trofimov down to earth, to bring him back to reality. She does this by pointing out that he is unable to afford a pair of decent galoshes.

No one pays any attention to Epihodov. They don't even say goodbye to him. He sees himself as an important person, entrusted with responsibilities and power. But to Yasha he is no one. Even now he has again made a fool of himself. Epihodov's action is to draw attention to himself. Yasha's action is to ridicule Epihodov.

Hints: Lopahin attracts attention by commanding Epihodov and checking and locking everything in an owner-like fashion. Ranevskaya wanders around the room, sits down, touches the furniture and the walls. Gaev turns from time to time to the window and quietly wipes away tears.

Event 4.18 (Leading Character Anya)

[Ranevskaya and Gaev remain alone. As though they had been waiting for this, they throw themselves on each other's necks, and sob quietly, with restraint, afraid of being overheard]

GAEV: *[In despair]* My sister, my sister!...

RANEVSKAYA: Oh, my sweet, my beautiful orchard!... My life, my youth, my happiness, goodbye!... goodbye!...

VOICE OF ANYA: *[Calling gaily]* Mamma!

VOICE OF TROFIMOV: *[Gaily, excitedly]* Aa-oo!

RANEVSKAYA: One last look at the walls, at the windows.... My dear mother loved to walk about this room....

GAEV: My sister, my sister!...

VOICE OF ANYA: Mamma!

VOICE OF TROFIMOV: Aa-oo!

157

RANEVSKAYA: We are coming! *[They go out]*

Mamma and uncle are distraught and unable to part with their old house. Conflict: Anya sees her uncle and mother as old-fashioned people who can't understand that there is nothing to grieve for, that ahead lies a new and happier life. But Ranevskaya and Gaev feel they have nothing more to expect from life: with the loss of their estate, life has lost all meaning for them. Anya's action is to encourage her mother and uncle and lead them forward. Ranevskaya's and Gaev's action is to conceal their emotions so as not to destroy Anya's radiant hopes.

Event 4.19 (Firs's Monologue)

> *[The stage is empty. There is the sound of doors being locked, then of the carriages driving away. There is silence. In the stillness there is the dull stroke of an axe in a tree, clanging with a mournful lonely sound. Footsteps are heard. Firs appears in the doorway on the right. He is dressed, as always, in a jacket and white waistcoat, with slippers on his feet. He is ill]*
>
> FIRS: *[Goes up to the doors and tries the handles]* Locked. They have gone.... *[Sits down on the sofa]* They have forgotten me.... Never mind.... I'll sit here a bit.... Leonid Andreyevich surely hasn't put his fur coat on and gone off in his thin overcoat.... *[Sighs anxiously]* I didn't see after him.... These foolish young people! *[Mutters something that cannot be distinguished]* Life has slipped by as though I hadn't lived. *[Lies down]* I'll lie down a bit.... There's no strength in you left, nothing left, nothing.... Ech! I'm good-for-nothing!... *[Lies motionless]*
>
> *[A sound is heard that seems to come from the sky, like a breaking harp string, dying away mournfully. All is still again, and there is heard nothing but the strokes of the axe far away in the orchard]*

As always, in a monologue we try to find juxtapositions, internal debate. The given circumstance here is that everyone has forgotten about the existence of Firs. He cannot accept the fact that no one needs him anymore. He tries to prove to himself that he is necessary, that without him the helpless and mindless Gaev will certainly be lost. On the other hand, he realizes that he no longer has the strength to perform his duties. So Firs concludes that there is no more meaning to his life. All that is left is to die.

PART THREE

The Superobjective of the Character

22. The Concept of the Superobjective

STANISLAVSKY POINTED OUT that every character in a play has a certain overall objective, or main desire, which determines his behavior throughout the play and imparts an integrated inner meaning to all his words, conflicts, and actions. Stanislavsky called that desire the *superobjective* of the character.

The concept of the superobjective lies at the root of Stanislavsky's entire system. According to Stanislavsky, without the superobjective the system does not exist. The striving toward the superobjective is what brings all parts of the role together, sets it on the right road, and determines its development in the direction given by the author. Knowledge of the character's superobjective makes it possible for both actor and director to create an integral and purposeful stage character and performance.

What is this superobjective of the character? To answer this question we must recall that the essence of each character is revealed through his interaction with other characters, through the conflicts in which he is involved. Each of these conflicts contributes to the superobjective of the character and is a step toward attaining his main desire. Hence, in order to understand the superobjective of the character it is necessary to trace a common thread in all his conflicts which ties them together in an integral whole.

As we know, in any conflict a character strives to impose a certain opinion about himself or his opponent. In either case this allows him to reveal himself and demonstrate what he is. The difference is that in the former case the character openly declares his opinion of himself, while in the latter he does this obliquely, revealing himself by his perception of his opponent. Thus the common thread passing through all the character's conflicts without exception, giving them uniform meaning, is a striving to impose a certain opinion of himself and, as a consequence, to be accepted in the manner he desires. In other words, *the superobjective of the character is how he wants to be perceived by all other characters of the play.*

*

Usually it is not easy to determine the superobjective of a given character. It is rarely possible to encompass an entire role and identify its superobjective without a detailed analysis of the play. Especially as in a good play the essence of a character unfolds gradually, and his main desire—superobjective—seeps out little by little throughout the entire play. Even in those cases where one can surmise the character's superobjective, there is no guarantee that the guess will prove to be correct.

Insofar as the superobjective of a character manifests itself in all his interactions with other characters without exception, the only systematic way to identify it is by studying the character's conflicts, actions, and words spoken in pursuance of them. In reviewing all the events involving a given character, we can detect a certain trend and see how the character wishes to be accepted by other characters of the play.

Knowledge of the superobjective is also extremely important because it makes it possible to verify the accuracy of the conflicts constructed while analyzing the play. This means that if in a particular event the character's behavior is not directed toward the achievement of an already identified superobjective or, even worse, contradicts it, then usually some mistake has been made in analyzing the given event.

23. *Superobjectives of* The Cherry Orchard *Characters*

Here we present the superobjectives of all the characters of *The Cherry Orchard* and show their connections with the preceding analyses of the play's events.

The Superobjective of Lopahin

A careful study of the role of Lopahin leads to the conclusion that throughout the play he strives to make people see him as a new master in life, a man of the future. That is his superobjective.

In order to confirm this conclusion, let us have another look at all the events involving Lopahin and see how his superobjective is reflected in them.

As a new master Lopahin demands the same treatment as the old gentry. In events E1.1 and E1.3 to E1.5 he reprimands the servants Dunyasha and Epihodov, who have gotten out of control, and in E1.18 he rebuffs Gaev, who attempts to slight him. He has acquired high-society manners (E1.27) and an enhanced style of living (E2.8) and has friendly relations with the nobleman Pishchik (E1.29, E3.19, E4.11). Lopahin is proud of his closeness to Ranevskaya (E1.21, E2.8) and sees himself as much a member of the family as the intellectual Trofimov (E2.11). He is an absolutely blameless person, a real gentleman (E2.19, E3.23, E4.4).

The new master Lopahin knows better than the old masters how to behave with ordinary folk. He keeps the worthless valet Yasha (E4.1) at arm's length, immediately puts an end to the pestering of the drunken Wayfarer (E2.17), and in E2.10, making fun of Firs, remarks that the only redeeming feature of the old times was that the people were kept in strict subjugation ("There was flogging at least").

In several events in Acts I and II Lopahin shows himself to be a person who keeps abreast of the times, who understands contemporary life much better than the old masters and knows exactly what to do in order to be successful (E1.22, E1.25, E1.29). Lopahin is a man of new, progressive ideas (E1.22); his success fully entitles him to teach Ranevskaya and Gaev, and their only salvation is to trust implicitly in his abilities and knowledge of life (E2.4, E2.6, E2.10). Finally, in E2.13 he unabashedly declares himself to be a giant, a man toiling tirelessly for the good of society.

In Act III Lopahin proclaims himself a victor, builder of a bright new life: "We will build houses... and our grandsons and great-grandsons will see a new life springing up there. Music! Play up!" In events E3.22 and E3.24 he speaks of himself as a person who has done the impossible and who, thanks to his abilities, has joined the ranks of the new masters of life: "Musicians, play up!... Here comes the new master!... I can pay for everything!" He points out to the weeping Ranevskaya that she has lost everything only because she failed to trust his abilities (E3.23).

Despite Lopahin's noble efforts to save Ranevskaya from ruin, her family ends all relations with him after the sale of the estate. But Lopahin continues to insist on his closeness to the Ranevskaya household. He is prepared to make the first step toward restoring their old relationship (E4.1, E4.2), but he immediately realizes that he has gone too far, that he has other plans in life, and that he can get on quite well without this house and without these people (E4.14). He is an important person who knows his worth (E4.3, E4.17); the future belongs to him. Lopahin reminds the others that soon his great plan will be implemented, and he barely bids Ranevskaya a parting farewell (E4.17).

The Superobjective of Ranevskaya

Ranevskaya sees herself as a person boundlessly devoted to her home and family, and she seeks to be perceived accordingly. Let us see how this superobjective manifests itself in the events involving her.

In the arrival scene (E1.6) and in the subsequent events E1.17 and E1.33, Ranevskaya emphasizes that the years apart have not distanced her from her home and family or in any way changed her attitude toward them. Everything here is memorable to her, and it is only here that she can reacquire happiness and peace of mind. Today she wants to be surrounded by her family (E1.20); strangers—Lopahin, Pishchik, and later Trofimov—only distract her and keep her away from her family (E1.21, E1.29, E1.32, E1.34). Quite naturally, she rejects Lopahin's outrageous proposal to destroy her beloved estate (E1.22, E1.29, and further, E2.4, E2.6, E2.13).

Ranevskaya hastens to declare that there is no going back to the past, that she has returned to her family for good (E1.23) and doesn't even wish to remember her life in Paris (E1.22). She is deeply repentant for her passion and sees herself as greatly punished for the ruin she has brought to her family (E1.35). Ranevskaya is concerned with the fate of the dowerless Varya (E1.31) and repeatedly tries to arrange her marriage to Lopahin (E2.8, E3.5, E4.13).

Throughout Act II Ranevskaya continues to insist that nothing is more important to her than home and family. She appeals to her brother for help in forgetting about her lover, who is again trying to tear her away from her family (E2.5, E2.7). She is frightened by the very thought of returning to him (E2.15). Only here, among people dear to her and on her beloved estate, can she be free of him for good. Furthermore, E2.16 and E2.18 characterize Ranevskaya as a loving mother and E2.17 as a guardian of old family tradition.

In Act III Ranevskaya is the only person who still expects and hopes to save the estate. She rallies the attention of oth-

ers to the fact that the fate of the family is being decided today (E3.2, E3.10 to E3.13). Unable to cope with the terror of
anticipation, she keeps Varya (E3.4) and Trofimov (E3.6) at
her side. Ranevskaya just barely tolerates the impertinent pestering of Pishchik (E3.14) and is indignant with Trofimov,
who has dared to remind her on such a terrible day in her life
that she herself has ruined her family (E3.7). The news that
her beloved estate will be destroyed plunges Ranevskaya into
profound grief (E3.22 to E3.25).

In Act IV Ranevskaya is incensed by the ugly behavior of
Lopahin, who has invaded their home and interferes with their
parting from the house (E4.1, E4.17), and by the indifference
toward her family displayed by Pishchik (E4.12). While they
have lost the house, Ranevskaya still has her family, and till the
end she is concerned with the fate of Varya and Firs (E4.13,
E4.15), and she strives not to dash Anya's hopes about a happy
future (E3.25, E4.9, E4.18). Although she will be leaving for
Paris, Ranevskaya is confident she will soon return (E4.9).

The Superobjective of Gaev

Gaev's superobjective is to be perceived as head of the clan,
responsible for preserving the family and its traditions and
spiritual values.

Anything that undermines the family's position, casts
blight on its good name, or runs contrary to its traditions
arouses his ire and opposition. Gaev is a principled opponent
of any interference in the existing order of things (E2.14),
and it is only natural that he indignantly rejects the proposal
to carve up the estate into cottage plots (E1.22, E2.6).

Gaev cannot tolerate even the mention of Ranevskaya's
shameful affair, which has led to the family's ruin (E1.23,
E2.7). He actively opposes Lopahin's efforts to become an accepted person in their home, seeing him as a vulgar money-
grubber, alien and hostile to his, Gaev's, world (E1.18, E1.25,
E2.4, E2.19, E3.20, E4.1, E4.17). The very thought that Varya

might marry Lopahin is anathema to Gaev (E1.30). Similarly, Gaev barely tolerates the presence of that brazen valet Yasha in the house (E1.38, E2.5, E4.9).

Gaev sees himself as bearing responsibility for preserving the household and the family and does all he can toward these ends. First he tries to confront his sister with the family's real state of affairs (E1.17, E1.33), then, realizing that Ranevskaya is totally absorbed with her personal problems, takes the task of salvaging the estate into his own hands (E1.39, E1.41, E2.9).

Gaev does all he can to lessen tensions within the family (E1.19, E1.40) or prematurely dash Anya's childish illusions regarding their future (E4.9, E4.18). To Gaev, Firs is an inalienable part of the household, and he patiently tolerates the old man's constant grumbling. Gaev is shocked when Charlotta, like Varya, parts with the family (E4.10), and to the very end he attempts to bring them all together and prevent the final collapse of their household (E4.16).

The Superobjective of Trofimov

Trofimov sees himself as the builder of a bright future, a new person standing above everything personal and material. That is his superobjective.

Trofimov is confident that he is out of the ordinary (E2.12, E4.3) and attracts the interest of others (E1.34, E1.36). He is independent (E1.43) and impervious to things shallow and vain (E3.8, E4.3).

Trofimov looks down on that primitive "predator" Lopahin (E2.11, E4.2, E4.3) and on Pishchik with his eternal quest for money (E3.1). He views that babbler Gaev with irony (E2.14) and ridicules the narrow-minded Varya who is incapable of rising above her philistine level (Act III). Trofimov counsels the blind, lost Ranevskaya (E3.2, E3.6) and opens her eyes to her errors (E3.7). Finally, in Act IV (E4.17) Trofimov acts as a leader guiding Ranevskaya's family toward a new life.

Trofimov is ready to sacrifice his love to assert himself as Anya's teacher and spiritual mentor. He cannot bring himself down to the level of common people or place himself in the trivial and ridiculous situation of a man in love (E2.20, E3.6).

The Superobjective of Anya

At seventeen Anya has entered a period of life when everything around her seems clear, and obvious answers exist to all questions. She considers herself an adult and independent person and strives to make this clear to everyone. That is her superobjective.

In E1.8 Anya indicates to Dunyasha that she no longer cares for her stupid prattle, that she now has more important concerns and duties. In E1.9 Anya flatly declares that she no longer requires anyone's supervision ("What did you want to burden me with Charlotta for?"). In E1.10 Anya tells Varya how to behave with Lopahin ("Why is it you don't come to an understanding? What are you waiting for?") and "opens her eyes" to Ranevskaya (E1.9, E1.14). Anya strives to be involved with the others in the affairs of the estate (E1.43); she considers herself responsible for her unhappy mother's fate (E2.16) and for the behavior of that inveterate babbler, her uncle (E1.19, E1.40, E1.42, E2.14, E4.16).

Anya, who is just entering life, sees it in greater breadth and depth than the older generation. She thinks Varya's dreams of the future are foolish (E1.11). She understands that the old way of life has come to an end (E2.20) and sees nothing sad about that (E3.10, E3.25). In Act IV Anya finally assumes all the functions of an adult member of the family. She rebukes Lopahin (E4.4), gives orders about the household (E4.5, E4.6), and in E4.9, E4.17, and E4.18 acts as a leader guiding the family into a new life.

The Superobjective of Varya

Varya considers herself the only person on whose shoulders lie all the concerns of the household and family. In accordance with this superobjective, Varya constantly emphasizes how busy she is and how she is responsible for everything happening in the house. This is clearly apparent starting with the scene of Ranevskaya's arrival (E1.6), when Varya informs her that her rooms have been preserved unchanged, and up to the very departure scene (E4.18), when Varya continues to look for an umbrella and galoshes. Even in the "proposal" scene (E4.14) Varya continues to show that her entrance was due to urgent household chores.

Throughout the play Varya insists that she is the sole supervisor of all household affairs. She keeps a constant eye on the unruly servants (E1.13, E1.38, E1.43, E3.17, E4.7), ejects unwanted guests on her own initiative (E1.20, E1.29), and considers herself entitled to rebuke Ranevskaya (E2.18) for her outrageous behavior and to reprove Trofimov (E1.34, E1.43). Varya is the only person in the family who understands the estate's true condition. From the beginning she knows that it cannot be saved (E1.9) and disregards the plans of that babbler Gaev (E1.39, E1.41, E1.43).

Varya is responsible for caring for the helpless Firs (E1.16, E4.6), the distraught Ranevskaya (E3.4), and for Anya, whom she sees as a naive child requiring patronage and help (E1.9 to E1.11, E1.14, E1.43, E4.6). Varya's concern for Anya (see E1.11) is a cause of constant spats with the pauper student Trofimov, to whom she continually points out that Anya is not for him and that he should leave her alone (E3.1, E3.4, E3.5, E4.3, E4.17).

Realizing that her personal life has failed, Varya tells Ranevskaya that all that is left for her is work (E3.5, E4.15).

The Superobjective of Dunyasha

Dunyasha repeatedly claims to be so fragile, unable to work, capricious, and high-strung—all qualities which, in her view, characterize a real young lady. Accordingly, her superobjective is to make people see her not as a rustic servant but as a "real young lady."

Dunyasha behaves too freely with Lopahin, not as a servant should (E1.1, E1.3, E1.5). Dunyasha is confident that she has the same interests as the young lady Anya (E1.8). After some brief doubts (E1.5), Dunyasha concludes that the clerk Epihodov is not suitable for her and subsequently treats him with capricious aloofness (E2.2, E3.16). Dunyasha is impressed by Yasha's "European" finesse and regards him as a young man who, at last, is suitable for her (E1.12). As Yasha's lover, Dunyasha, like a respectable girl, constantly demands appropriate treatment (E2.3, E3.15, E4.8).

The Superobjective of Yasha

After living for five years abroad, Yasha understands that he has become an entirely different person and no longer belongs to the place where he was born and grew up. Accordingly, Yasha's superobjective is to make people realize that he has nothing to do with common folk.

This is readily seen in all events involving Yasha. He "doesn't recognize" Dunyasha during their first meeting (E1.12), and later, when he is her lover, he keeps stressing the distance between them and saying that she is not suitable for him (E2.3, E3.15, E4.8). Everyone and everything in the house irritate Yasha (E3.13). He despises Epihodov (E2.2, E4.17) and Firs (E3.9) and doesn't even wish to see his own mother (E1.38, E4.7). Yasha is Ranevskaya's right-hand man (E1.26, E2.5, E3.11), and, naturally, his place now is not in the servants' quarters but with the gentlefolk with whom he feels himself to be all but equal (E1.38, E2.5, E3.13, E4.5). Finally, in E4.1, he talks with Lopahin with the air of a man who is well aware of his own worth.

The Superobjective of Firs

Everyone treats Firs condescendingly and patronizingly. People see him as an old man whose life is over and whose retirement is long overdue. Firs, however, believes it is too early to discount him. He is still needed around the house because his experience is absolutely essential. Thus Firs's superobjective is to be seen as a wise, irreplaceable person on whom the entire household must rely. This desire is easily traceable through all the events involving him.

The Superobjective of Pishchik

Pishchik sees himself as a nice fellow, everyone's friend, and wants to be perceived as such by others. He is the soul of any company, a man who knows how to behave in any circumstance (E1.22, E1.26, E3.3, E3.24). He is everyone's friend (E4.11, E4.12), everyone likes him (E3.1), and no one can turn him down (E1.32, E1.37, E3.15).

The Superobjective of Charlotta

The governess Charlotta sees herself as an independent woman who is above the conventionalities of life, and she strives for those around her to perceive her likewise.

Charlotta violates every standard of behavior of a governess in the house. She is uninvolved in the excitement of welcoming Ranevskaya home (E1.7) and is not interested in the company of either gentlefolk (E1.28) or servants (E2.2), preferring to go hunting. She jokes boldly with the clumsy Lopahin (E1.27), the thick-skinned Pishchik (E3.3), and the stupid Epihodov (E2.2). Charlotta keeps her emotions in check and without hesitation leaves the Ranevskaya household, even though she is no longer young and has nothing to look forward to: she sings a ditty and shows a new trick (E4.10).

The Superobjective of Epihodov

Epihodov considers himself an important person deserving every respect. Accordingly, he demands that others perceive him so. But people are incapable of judging Epihodov on his merits: they do not notice his presence and constantly belittle him.

In events E1.4 and E4.17 Epihodov manages to make his presence noted. In E2.2 he forcibly makes himself the center of attention, ignoring Charlotta's ironic comments and Yasha's and Dunyasha's deliberate indifference. In E3.16 he accuses Dunyasha of not giving him due attention ("It's as if I were some insect"), and in a scene with Varya (E3.17) he insists that he can only "be judged by persons of understanding and my elders." Accordingly, in E4.5 Epihodov totally ignores Anya's orders.

24. On Staging a Play

When a true artist creates a dramatic work, he is always inspired by certain ideas, feelings, and experiences of life. To convey his perception of the world to an audience, the author builds in his imagination a cast of characters with their pasts, presents, and futures, with their own psychologies, motivations, and conflicts. With the example of their lives and mutual relationships, the author seeks to lead the audience to certain conclusions and to awake appropriate emotions and reactions.

When a director stages a play, he is not necessarily trying to discover the author's ideas, especially since no one can say for sure that he understands the author. A director chooses a play because in it he finds material which may be used to express his own ideas and perceptions of life.

But not every director's idea may be successfully "grafted" onto a given play. Any idea not based on the circumstances presented by the author leads to distortion of the relationships between characters and a butchering of the author's text. New circumstances proposed by the director give rise to new relationships and character traits that cannot be justified by the text of the play.

Conclusion

THE METHOD DISCUSSED in this book is not a form of literary criticism which seeks to interpret the play or, in other words, to discover the author's intent, analyze the themes and ideas in the play, explain its characters and plot situations, determine its historical, social, and literary contexts, and so forth. The method of working on the play and the role has a direct and practical purpose: to provide an actor with a concrete technique of finding the relationships between the characters and determining their behavior during each moment of their stage existence. Employing the method properly, an actor begins to use the logic of his character and view other characters through his character's eyes, entering into conflicts with the others and upholding his character's point of view. A process of internal merging of the actor and his character occurs. This inner transformation is reflected in the external behavior of the character: the actor physically acquires the body and body language of another person. Thus the internal helps the external, and the external, in turns, facilitates the development of the internal, enhancing penetration into the psychology of the character. Eventually there comes a moment when the actor subconsciously develops the traits of another person, intuition and feeling come into play which keep the actor from pretending and lead instead to natural reactions, to a natural life on the stage.

"From the conscious to the subconscious, from the deliberate to the spontaneous" is Stanislavsky's formula. From a conscious construction of the role, from the re-creation of the inner logic of the character's behavior to emotions—not the other way around. It is impossible to create a purposeful and natural character guided by guesswork, intuition, and fortuitous interpretation of the play and the role.

The naturalness of an actor's existence on the stage causes the audience to believe and arouses its spontaneous reaction. Spontaneous communication between the actor and the audience occurs: the actor emotionally affects the audience, whose reaction, in turn, inspires the actor. Only such performance, only such theater which can evoke the thoughts and feelings of the audience—only such theater can be called emotional.

Appendix I. Ranevskaya's and Lopahin's Age

Although Chekhov does not mention Ranevskaya's age, *The Cherry Orchard* contains several indications that she is about forty-five years old.

a. Ranevskaya is younger than Gaev, who is fifty-one. In E1.19 Gaev, speaking to Anya, says: "How like you are to your mother! *[To his sister]* At her age you were just the same, Lyuba." As a rule, such comments are addressed to a younger person rather than the other way around.

b. In E2.10 eighty-seven-year-old Firs says to Ranevskaya, "They were arranging my wedding before your papa was born." In the first third of the nineteenth century, marriage at seventeen was quite normal. Let us assume that Firs's marriage was arranged when he was seventeen. Hence Gaev's father could not have been born more than seventy years before. If he married at seventeen, by the beginning of the play his oldest child could not be older than fifty-two, which is just about how old Gaev is. Thus Ranevskaya is his younger sister.

c. In E4.17 Gaev reminisces, "I remember when I was six years old sitting in this window on Trinity Day watching my father going to church...." Trinity is one of the most important Russian religious holidays. That Gaev's father was going to church without his wife indicates some extraordinary event that has kept her home. This event could have been the birth of Gaev's sister. It would explain not only why Gaev has retained the day in his memory but also why he is recalling it at this time, when he and his sister are being forced out of the house in which they were born and grew up. Hence Ranevskaya is six years younger than her brother, or forty-five years old.

The only direct suggestion of Lopahin's age is given in E1.2, when he recalls how Ranevskaya, who was "still young and slim," brought him into the house to wash and console him. From the text of the play, Lopahin was fifteen at the time. Assuming that Ranevskaya was twenty-three to twenty-five, it would lead to the conclusion that in the play Lopahin is thirty-five to thirty-seven years old.

It is interesting to note that in the first version of the play[14] Lopahin speaks of himself as "a kid of five or six." Thus initially Lopahin was nine or ten years younger, or about the same age as Trofimov. That would explain their mutual jealousy and also their use, when addressing each other, of the informal second-person-singular "thou."

Appendix II. *Tolstoy's Poem, The Sinful Woman*

In the course of Event 3.8, the Station Master stands in the middle of the room and recites several lines from Alexey K. Tolstoy's poem *The Sinful Woman*. Apparently this poem (c. 1857) has never been translated into English, but even in Russia no one remembers it nowadays.

The poem is based on an episode from the New Testament in which a sinful woman is converted through her encounter with Christ. The poem begins with the description of a luxurious feast in a wealthy home in Palestine. The guests discuss a stranger who teaches humility and forgiveness and whose glance "no one has been able yet to withstand." A beautiful courtesan is tempted by pride publicly to challenge the powers of the stranger. Her challenge is answered soon, for Christ, humble and simple, approaches the crowd. He does not speak but only fixes his eyes upon the woman. A miraculous conversion takes place in the woman's heart. She suddenly understands the wickedness of her life, and, crying, she falls at Christ's feet. Without uttering a word, Christ converts the woman to a new life.

In Chekhov's time this poem was widely known, and only a few lines were needed to refer the audience to its familiar plot and characters. This reference emphasizes the comical effect of the preceding scene where, contrary to the miraculous conversion of the sinner, the new apostle of truth, Petya Trofimov, falls down the stairs while fleeing in horror from

Ranevskaya, whose eyes he has tried to open to her errors and delusions.

Appendix III. Exploring the Method in the Workshop Environment

Purpose: To gain an understanding of the main theoretical principles we have discussed and use them in a "hands-on," practical situation. This is accomplished through the performance of selected scenes in the workshop environment. Below we list our recommendations for choosing these scenes, and for approaching their realization on stage.

Prerequisites: It is desirable for students to have had a basic acting class or equivalent training. The workshop participants must be familiar with the play.

Basic Concepts and Terminology

Before the workshop participants can work on specific scenes (events), they should be acquainted with the concepts and terms employed. Students should understand the basic principle of the method: that each character of the play is involved in a continuous series of personal confrontations or conflicts with other characters. The conflicts are always based on the characters' perceptions of one another. This means that, as a result of some circumstances, one of the characters forms an opinion about himself or his opponent which in turn causes the latter to disagree. It is important to emphasize that the character's conflicts are defined entirely by the circumstances given by the author. Then the students are introduced to the concepts of leading character, led character, and aspects of the conflict.

Work on Selected Events

Our selection includes the following twelve events: E1.3 to E1.5, E1.8, E1.12, E1.38, E2.2, E2.3, E3.15, E3.16, E4.1, and E4.8. We recommend starting with events E1.8, E1.12, E2.3, and E3.15, which were analyzed in detail in Part One (Examples I to IV). A specific procedure should be followed during the work on an event. Here is an example of the procedure using E1.8.

a. Analysis of the Event

1. The work on an event begins with a discussion of the life circumstances of the characters involved in the event.

2. In order to determine the conflict, it is first necessary to identify the leading character. The student must examine the text of the event and decide who is the active character, the striving party. In E1.8 the leading character is Dunyasha.

3. All workshop participants, in a common effort, search for the circumstance that leads to a personal confrontation between the characters. As a rule, this circumstance can be found either immediately before an event or in its very beginning. The circumstance must be presented as it is seen through the eyes of the leading character, in his own interpretation. Students should remember that this interpretation must be based on the material of the play and not on one's unrestricted imagination.

In Event 1.8 such a circumstance is Anya's return home after an absence of several months. Using everything that is known about Dunyasha, students must try to understand how she perceives this circumstance. For instance, Dunyasha's response to Anya's arrival might be expressed in these words: "Finally, my loneliness is over! I am going mad from boredom. Anya is the only person I can seek advice from or unburden my heart to." Thus Dunyasha's reaction to Anya's arrival, in itself, contains Dunyasha's budding opinion of Anya.

Then one searches for given circumstances which would enrich Dunyasha's perception of Anya. The more circumstances are found, the more precisely and fully Dunyasha's position in the conflict will be characterized. For example, "Anya, the mistress's daughter, is approximately the same age as Dunyasha. They grew up together, and Anya does not treat Dunyasha like

178

a servant but like a member of the family. She stays abreast of all developments in Dunyasha's life and knows all her love secrets." All this leads to a generalization that to Dunyasha, Anya is not just a mistress but a person who is close to her and with whom she has much in common.

Dunyasha's outlook is the cause of the confrontation between the characters in E1.8. Thus we should refer to Anya's circumstances and find among them those that will not allow her to agree with Dunyasha. As in Dunyasha's case, we search for those of Anya's circumstances that reveal how she perceives herself. For example, "Anya is in a state of great distress which has driven her to insomnia. After five years of separation Anya brings home her unhappy, lost, and helpless mother. The family's fate is in limbo; they are broke and any day may lose the beautiful estate. Anya is fully immersed in family problems which are not relevant to Dunyasha and which Anya would never share with a maid." In other words, Anya's inner world has nothing in common with Dunyasha's. This determines her position in the conflict in the given event.

b. Search for the Actions

It is not sufficient to determine the conflict within an event. An actor must be able to deliver his side of the conflict to his partner and ultimately to the audience. To make his position clear, an actor resorts to a specific tactic of behavior or action.

The student must clearly understand that an action is not a simple physical movement but a complex psycho-physical process happening over a period of time. While performing their actions, actors spontaneously create mise-en-scènes and make use of the set and props.

To determine the character's actions, students should reread the event and, on the basis of the conflict already identified and the characters' words and the author's stage directions, try to understand the character's behavior in the event, what tactic he uses to impose his position on his opponent in the conflict. When the verbal expressions of actions are found, students should immediately try to perform these actions on stage, clarifying and, if necessary, changing them.

In the first stage of work on a scene, students should not use the author's text or memorize it. They should use their own words which are comfortable but similar in meaning. For example:

> DUNYASHA: Let me look at you, I have missed you greatly! And you? Did you think of me often? I've spent sleepless nights waiting for you! So much has happened, you would not even guess!
>
> ANYA: Wait a minute, Dunyasha.... I'm so tired...I hardly slept. Thank God, I'm home at last!

Naturally, each performer finds his own words, convenient for him. But the words should be consistent with the given conflict and action.

The degree of mastery of an action is directly related to repetition. To strengthen an ability to fix action and the author's text, students should repeatedly return to performing a given event. Be sure that the students do not lose actions already acquired.

*

The other eleven events should be worked on following the same procedure: the leading character is identified; a circumstance which forces the leading character toward personal confrontation with other characters is found; the positions of the leading and led characters are determined; and the character's actions are sought and refined on the stage. The found relationships between characters should not differ in principle from those given in the descriptions of the corresponding conflicts in Part Two. To help the students, here are the circumstances which stimulate the leading character to confrontation in the selected events:

E1.3: At any moment the mistress, Ranevskaya, who has been abroad for five years, will be back in the house.

E1.4: Epihodov winds up alone with Lopahin.

E1.5: Lopahin scolds Dunyasha for her appearance and behavior.

E1.12: Valet Yasha has returned home after being abroad for five years, in Paris.

E1.38: Gaev starts to discuss Ranevskaya in the presence of her valet.

E2.2: Today Epihodov winds up in the same company with Dunyasha, who lately has stopped paying him any attention.

E2.3: Dunyasha has entered into a love affair with Yasha, but he has not proposed to her.

E3.15: Dunyasha is an active participant in her mistress's ball.

E3.16: Dunyasha is constantly avoiding Epihodov.

E4.1: Yasha, once again, is leaving for Paris.

E4.8: Yasha, who is leaving for Paris, pays no attention to Dunyasha.

Reminder: The student must present these circumstances using the leading character's point of view, thus discovering his logic and way of thinking.

Superobjectives of the Characters

The twelve events chosen by us include most of the scenes in the play involving Yasha and Dunyasha. This allows the use of these events for the study of the superobjective of the character. In order to find the superobjective, the character's behavior, conflicts, and words must be closely observed. Then one must conclude what the character's concept of himself is and how he wishes to be perceived by all other characters of the play (see Part Three). In determining Dunyasha's superobjective, the following events are used: E1.3 to E1.5, E1.8, E1.12, E2.2 to E2.3, E3.15, E3.16, and E4.8. To determine Yasha's superobjective, use E1.12, E1.38, E2.2 to E2.3, E3.15, E4.1, and E4.8. Students may also find it useful to read in Part Two descriptions of the additional events involving Yasha

(E2.5, E3.9, E3.11, E3.13, E4.5, E4.6, E4.17) and Dunyasha (E1.1) which were not considered in the workshop. The found superobjectives of Yasha and Dunyasha should be compared with their superobjectives given in Part Three.

Then the students should act out E1.8, E2.3, E3.15, and E4.8 again, this time taking into consideration the found superobjectives of the characters. These scenes should be run through with the same cast so that they may be seen as a part of a performance.

BIBLIOGRAPHY

1. Konstantin Stanislavsky, *An Actor Prepares*. New York, Theatre Arts Books, 1967.

2. Konstantin Stanislavsky, *Building a Character*. New York, Routledge/Theatre Arts Books, 1989.

3. Konstantin Stanislavsky, *Creating a Role*. New York, Theatre Arts Books, 1961.

4. Nikolai Kovshov, *Uroki M. N. Kedrova*. Moscow, Iskusstvo, 1983 (in Russian).

5. Mikhail Kedrov, *Stat'i, rechi, besedy, zametki*. Moscow, Vseros. teatr. o-vo, 1978 (in Russian).

6. Vladimir Prokof'ev, "O rezhesserskoi rabote Kedrova nad spektaklem *Plody prosveshchen'ia* L. Tolstogo," *Yearbook of the Moscow Art Theatre (1951–52)*. Moscow, Iskusstvo, 1956 (in Russian).

7. Vasilii Toporkov, "Moia rabota nad rol'iu professora Kruglosvetova," *Yearbook of the Moscow Art Theatre (1951–52)*. Moscow, Iskusstvo, 1956 (in Russian).

8. Georgii Tovstonogov, *The Profession of the Stage-Director*. Moscow, Progress Publishers, 1972.

9. Georgii Tovstonogov, *Zerkalo stseny*. 2 vols. Leningrad, Iskusstvo, Leningradskoe otdelenie, 1984 (in Russian).

10. Georgii Tovstonogov, *Besedy s kollegami: popytka osmysleniia rezhisserskogo opyta*. Moscow, STD RSFSR, 1988 (in Russian).

11. Valentina Ryzhova, *Put'k spektakliu*. Moscow, Iskusstvo, 1967 (in Russian).

12. "Tovstonogov repetiruet," *Teatr*, May 1983, pp. 45–58 (in Russian).

13. Maurice Valency, *The Breaking String*. New York, Oxford University Press, 1966.

14. Konstantin Stanislavsky, *Rezhesserskie ekzempliary K. S. Stanislavskogo, 1898–1930.* vol. 3. Moscow, Iskusstvo, 1983 (in Russian).

INDEX

Action, 15–16; description of, 35; identification of, 20; physical realization of, 21, 39, 179–180

Character: leading, *see* Leading side; led, *see* Led side; re-creation of logic of, 9–10, 173–174; secondary, 32
Circumstances. *See* Given circumstances.
Conflict, 15, 177; aspects of, 26–27; behavioral tactic in, *see* Action; concealed behind the text, 28, 36; focal point of, 16; incidental, *see* Incidental conflict; main, *see* Main conflict; sides of, 16, 36; three types of, 38; two types of relations in, 27, 37, 162

Event, 28; compared with a scene, 29; framework of, 37; interrupted, *see* Interrupted event; segmentation of a play into, 29, 37

Garnett, Constance, 12
Given circumstances, 17; presented from the character's standpoint, 18, 37, 45, 178; selection of, 18, 178–179
Group, 30

Ibsen, Henrik, 29
Incidental conflict, 32
Interrupted event, 34–35

Kedrov, Mikhail, 11

Leading side, 16, 19, 30; identification of, 19
Led side, 16, 30; different positions in a conflict, 30; involved in incidental conflict, 32, 37
Literary criticism and actors, 173

Main conflict, 32
Method of active analysis, 11
Monologue, 35–36, 37; danger of becoming lifeless, 36

Play: director's idea of, 172; memorizing text of, 39, 180; as struggle between characters, 15; as succession of events, 29

Shakespeare, William, 29
Stanislavsky, Konstantin: later findings of, 11; on verbal definition of actions, 35
Stanislavsky system: aim of, 9, 174; and superobjective, 13, 161; two parts of, 10
Superobjective of the character, 13, 161–162; determination of, 162, 181; verification of conflicts by, 162–163

Tartuffe (Molière), 11
Tolstoy, Alexey K., *The Sinful Woman*, 176
Tovstonogov, Georgii, 11

Williams, Tennessee, 29

A NOTE ON THE AUTHORS

Irina Levin was born in St. Petersburg, Russia, where she worked for thirteen years as an actress in repertory theatres, performed solo dramatic reading programs, and worked as a drama teacher and director at a theater studio. Since her emigration to the United States in 1976, she has conducted an audition class in New York, taught acting courses at Catholic University, and staged *Heart of a Dog* by Mikhail Bulgakov (1984, Washington, D.C.). Igor Levin is a mathematician; he holds a Ph.D. in computer science.